D1593469

A Well-Designed Business®
—THE POWER TALK FRIDAY EXPERTS VOL. 2—

LUANN NIGARA & FRIENDS

LuAnn Nigara
34 East Northfield Road
Livingston, NJ 07039
LuAnnNigara.com

info@luannnigara.com

ISBN: 978-1-7360915-0-0 (print)
ISBN: 978-1-7360915-1-7 (ebook)

Front and Back Cover Design – Nicole Heymer, Owner & Creative Director at Curio Electro
Front Photo Credit: Irina Leoni

Ordering Information:
Special discounts are available on quantity purchases by corporations, associations, and others.
For details, contact info@luannnigara.com.

Thank you, thank you, thank you.

I am thrilled beyond words we are on this journey together. Thank you for listening, for learning, for growing, and for sharing your time and your heart with me.

LuAnn

Contents

LuAnn Nigara

On my podcast, A *Well-Designed Business®*, I often make analogies to sports and restaurants. These are two of my favorite activities. At the core of each is the connection to other people. I live for the comradery—whether it is the laughing faces over the clink of glasses and silverware or the crack of the bat over the roar of the crowd. It's the conversations, it's the sharing, it's uniting together for a cause. It is lifting each other up every day, in every way.

I have always enjoyed sports—competitions of all kinds, really. And while I am very much a "workout by myself person," I love "playing with the team." The hours spent logging miles in the pool or on the bike or on the road are the work. The games, the time with teammates, that is the play. I always spent hours apart, in addition to the hours with any team I was on, practicing my skills, getting better at the mechanics. I was always "preparing to get lucky." You've heard me say that one a few times too. I knew the solo hours enabled me to show up and be a better contributor to the team.

In hindsight, I have realized, this is similar to the evolution of the *Power Talk Friday Experts* books.

Hours spent creating content for the podcast, for the books, for speaking engagements are like swimming, running, and biking. I do them solo, and I am quite happy doing just that. But where was the team, the playtime, and the fun? For me, it's in the book.

Month after month, meeting dozens and dozens of people, I found I was connecting on a different level with some. Every one of these coauthors has expressed a true desire to uplift you, the business owner in my audience. They get you, and they get what I am trying to do. I didn't explain it to them. I didn't say, "Hey, if you think like this, you can return to PTF again, or you can be part of the book." No, each one, in his/her own way, made it known to me they were energized and excited to teach you. They have a drive to share as much as they can with you, to help you be better.

Team culture.

My culture.

Our culture.

Just like when you hire employees. Several candidates may have the proper credentials and are perfectly qualified. But some will have the spark you want, that can-do attitude. They see your vision, and they want to do whatever they can to support it and to make it even better. They want to work with you to achieve it, and they make it known to you.

Ultimately and somewhat selfishly, these books are my way of putting a team together. We work together, over and over throughout the year. These are the men and women I invite to coach at my PTF events. These are the men and women I invite to speak at LuAnn Live and to teach at LuAnn University. These are the men and women I get to know so well that when you need a coach, I can recommend the right one without reservation. This is my team. They give to me, they give to you. I include them, I credit them, and I thank them because they joyfully bring the energy and focus to lift us all up.

Like the coauthors in the first volume, each of these rock stars is here to teach us her best practices, skills, and ideas on how to improve our businesses. These women have reached a place where they can turn to you with their reflections on work and success...lessons they have learned through their education, their triumphs, and their failures. Each chapter contains their personal blueprint with how it worked for them and why it will work for you. Stories of turning points, of hard lessons, of regrouping, and of going for their dreams.

There are two important takeaways I want you to consider as you read this book. The first is the magic comes when we honor ourselves and our employees along our journey in business and in life. Knowing who you are, what you want, whom you serve, and how you do it is the nonnegotiable first step. Chapter one, Book one: *The Making of A Well-Designed Business®*. Establish your mission and core values. Please do not skip over this.

The second is that I hope this book teaches you that none of us escapes the failures. We don't win every game. No matter what our Instagram "life" looks like, we all fail, often. But this is a good thing! If you are failing, you are in the game, you are doing. You've heard me say dozens of times, "If you don't want to make a mistake today, stay in bed." So, if you want to eliminate failure, don't play. But if you don't play, you also eliminate any possibility of success. Success requires participation. Participation requires risk. Both failure and success are found in the risk. Don't be afraid of this. This is good. This is where the fun is.

One of my favorite Wayne Dyer quotes is, "It is never crowded along the extra mile." Reading this as a preteen impacted me tremendously. You can't reach the "extra" mile if you haven't run the other miles before it. It taught me to do the work and then do more work because often others will not, and this will make all the difference in the world.

The same applies to our businesses. Entrepreneurism is hardly easy. I have learned it requires a daily decision. This is why I end every show with "Decide to Be Excellent." It is not a platitude. When it feels hard, you have a choice. You can choose to get in the game again. As you read this book, think about how happy and fulfilled you are when you have overcome an obstacle, mastered a new skill, or persevered through adversity. All those moments are found at the extra mile.

One last tip before you jump into the book. Do you remember Natasa Jones' episode, #570? Natasa shared her note-taking process for getting the most ROI out of every conference or seminar she attends. I know your head is going to spin with so many incredible ideas as you read this book, and I want you to maximize the benefits to your business. The simplicity of Natasa's process is genius. Here's how she does it.

Natasa starts with a new notebook, which she divides into five sections:

- To do now
- To do later
- To buy or download
- Mindset
- Follow up

As you read each chapter, with every, *Aha!*, every lesson that hits you, take an action. Write it in your notebook. If Eileen inspires you to honor an employee with a special one-on-one meeting or Kim's information nudges you to call your bookkeeper or Jamie reminds you your contract needs updating, list these in "To do now."

Maybe Desi or Amber spark something that flips a switch on an old pattern that you have been repeating. Make a note in "Mindset," and be sure to address it.

Possibly Amanda's message will spur you to start that IG Live series you've been thinking about or Sara's tremendous results with her systems persuade you it is finally time to create processes in your business. Note these in "To do later."

Darla mentions a book that motivated her at the start of her career and Sandra uses specific tools and apps to manage her business. Maybe you want to use these as well. Note them in "To buy or download."

And finally, "Follow up." The big one. Reading books, listening to podcasts, taking organized notes. It's all for nothing if we don't follow up. You must take the next steps.

You know that. I know you do.

Now, I want you to join me. Together, I want us to crowd that extra mile. Let's create a traffic jam like no other industry has seen. Imagine yourself there, looking left and right, all of us, going the extra mile in our businesses. Every interior designer, window-treatment specialist, architect, builder, landscape architect, web developer, photographer, writer, consultant—each of us helping, inspiring, encouraging each other to dig deeper, to learn more, to create more, to be more. Let's all run long past when others have stopped. Do the work. Success isn't unknowable. It isn't some crazy algorithm on social media. There isn't a certain amount of it, reserved for the few. It is yours for the doing. Not the taking, the doing.

Let's do this. We are a team.

See you at the extra mile!

Section One

Insights From Insiders

CHAPTER 1

Sandra Funk

I t has been my great pleasure to watch Sandra Funk literally transform her business into the well-oiled machine that it is today. On the podcast, I have shared with you many times how, at our very first meeting more than 10 years ago, Sandra impressed me as a standout among the other interior designers with whom I had worked during the previous 20-plus years through Window Works. Sandra was notably organized and thorough. I even remember thinking she was pretty darn knowledgeable about window treatments. You might think that is a funny notion, an odd impression to have or even to care about, especially when the point was to rely on me for that knowledge, as the expert Sandra had called in to advise her about window treatments. What it conveyed to me was the attention to detail in the way she runs her firm—a trait I would continue to notice in her over and over as the months and years passed.

Sandra has improved, grown, and pivoted her business, ultimately creating a duplicatable and profitable business. You know what I tell you all the time on the podcast: If you do not have a set of finite, repeatable, duplicatable processes in place for every aspect of your firm, you don't have a business, you have a "you." Well, Sandra most definitely has a business—a business she has shaped, formed, and created to support her ideals, her values, her clients, her employees, and her lifestyle.

I am excited for you to go on this chapter's journey with Sandra. As you do, keep in mind that while Sandra never wings it when it comes to running her business, that does not mean that she hasn't made mistakes, that she hasn't had failures, or that she hasn't had disappointments as an entrepreneur. It is important for you to know that none of us escapes the hard lessons or the hard moments that we face as entrepreneurs. The differentiator between success and lack of success is how we handle the setbacks.

If you want to be successful, there is one simple but not-so-easy action to take in the face of a setback or a flat-out failure. Start with a hard look in the mirror. Next, find your inner voice—your goddess voice—and listen to her carefully because she is telling you what you already knew was wrong. Then, seek information and productive criticism, preferably from someone whose opinion you value and trust. Finally, you must have the courage to know what your nonnegotiables are. Decide what your business will be, what it means to you, what is the culture of your company, who are the clients you will work with and serve. With this powerful combination of your inner voice, informed, trusted advice, and your clear values and ideals, you can get to work creating your company road map.

This is exactly what Sandra did, and I couldn't be happier for her or prouder of her for it.

–LN

How and When to Charge for Joy and Profit

Sandra Funk

Understanding our client's *emotions* throughout a design project is everything. Once you have that approach in hand, the rest of the process becomes easier. Consider it an "aha" moment. And I had one too.

Changing my business structure based on my client's emotions was not optional. It was the *only* way for my interior design business to survive.

First, me: exhausted and riddled with anxiety

I *hated* charging hourly. Yet, there I was, curled up in a small ball under my desk (metaphorically, but literally headed for it quite soon), vowing to never send another time bill. I was exhausted by all of the tracking, documenting, editing, revising, and positioning of my design fees.

You know that soul-crushing day that invoices are due to go out? You're hitting "send" on those emails and waiting for the sky to fall. Waiting for the inevitable responses that follow, like, "How could it have possibly taken that long?" and "How much more is to come?" Never mind if you are well within the estimate provided. It's *emotionally difficult* to receive constant invoices, no matter how well you prepare a client.

Second, clients: confused, overwhelmed, and dropping like flies

I hung up the phone and looked across the airport waiting area at LuAnn Nigara in disbelief. My client had just pulled the plug on their project. They were overwhelmed by multiple invoices

11

of design fees rolling in when they hadn't yet seen any design work. To them, the whole process felt out of control, maybe even suspicious.

The timing, the numbers, the unknown, all were too much for not just one, but *three* clients to handle. The desertion was my dark night of the soul. My wake-up call: my structure needed to change.

LuAnn and I were headed home from a conference together, so of course, I discussed my woes with my dear friend and mentor. The bottom line with LuAnn is always, "Where did you drop the ball? Where could you have set better expectations, been clearer, or just *done better?*" Obviously, I could do better. And so it began.

Looking back, I wasn't really putting myself in my client's shoes. When I think about what I want when I kick off a project, I have a pretty clear understanding of what makes me feel comfortable, in control, and taken care of. But my clients have their own views about the projects.

For instance, we did some landscaping for a client—design, grading, plants, adding sprinklers, and lighting. Lots of contractors and lots of quotes to wrangle. Here's what I noticed about my preferences:

- I want everything in writing.
- I want excellent communication. There is nothing more frustrating than chasing down someone to whom you've given business.
- I want a flat fee or an hourly estimate for the design or general contracting work.
- I want a ballpark figure on what the total job will cost at the very beginning, not after I pay the fee and spend the time working out the design with the client.

- I want a firm total cost of the project prior to any work starting.
- I want to know 100 percent of the costs up front—no surprise invoices or sneaky fees at the end.
- I want to be in control of the project scope and my money.

Why should I treat my clients any differently? So, I stopped right there and revamped my entire business structure. I literally stopped taking on new projects for three months; hired a business strategist, coach, and lawyer; and dug into a new way. I refused to sign one more client under the old structure.

I needed to rethink my future in the design business and I went back to my early experience and education to figure it out.

I come from a family of entrepreneurs and "makers." Michigan-born and -bred, I have DIY in my DNA. I was raised looking for ways to improve just about everything. We did most things ourselves and loved every minute of it.

I knew I would own my own business one day, so I got a degree in finance—you know, so I could handle all the money :). Still not sure of my calling, I went into business process consulting where I honed my obsession with making everything better. I was trained to look at any process for inefficiencies or synergies to improve, improve, improve.

I worked for amazing, talented designers before going out on my own. I also learned from teachers, coaches, courses, and conferences along the way. I proudly consider myself a lifelong student. I bring my natural way of turning everything that I do into a process. And, with my process consulting training, I've never been tied to a "how it's always been done" mentality, which I see as the enemy of innovation.

I was forced to take a long, hard look at my business and how it could improve. Once I nailed down the system and tested it, I felt compelled to share it. I want to see the entire industry improve. My program, the "Interior Design Standard," is how. It's my entire process, every system, template, and detail, including my flat-fee calculator and design agreement. You can find out more at www. houseoffunk.com/trade.

The Client's Emotional Timeline

I repeat: Understanding the client's *emotional* timeline throughout a design project is *everything*.

You and I know that we can clarify and clarify and estimate and remind but, sometimes, people only hear what they want to hear. In my case, I was communicating and setting expectations, but I wasn't structuring my projects to take my client's emotions into account.

I had over a decade in business and was a published award winner. I'd earned the right to charge $225 an hour, and got hired with that stated rate along with the associated fee estimates. The reality, however, was that my clients could not handle getting those multiple invoices. I'm a systems queen, so time billings went out every two weeks come hell or high water. That schedule meant that I didn't consider the timing of their arrival into the client's emotional project journey.

What the hell is a "client emotional project journey," you ask? It's the waves of excitement, hesitation, joy, anxiety, frustration, and then hope and joy again, that happen throughout the design process. I'll walk you through it—and, yes, it's the same for every client, just to somewhat different degrees depending on your ability to set expectations and walk a prospect through the process. And the client's own personality, of course.

Project Timeline and Payment Structure

The project timeline and payment structure means, simply put, taking a client's emotions into account. When your process is clear, efficient, and repeatable, you have more time to do what you do best: design.

First, you want to position your project structure strategically, according to the *emotional* timeline of a design client.

The most important thing I've learned is to talk real numbers right from the start. Yes, you'll scare a few away. Excellent! Those are ones who don't belong on your client list. Those prospects who can handle the honest numbers for your location and level of design are in the right place.

Here's how to do that: Give your potential client your flat design fee, a preliminary design idea, as well as a ballpark furnishing investment estimate (commonly known as a budget) to make sure that you're in the same stratosphere. (You and your client will set the actual furnishing investment estimate (FIE) together in the Conceptual Design Phase.) With that approach, clients feel respected, educated, and in control of their options. They can assess if they can afford you right from the start.

If it's a yes, a signed design agreement and 50 percent payment of the flat design fee kick off the project. The client feels excited to create a memorable and beautiful home.

That part is truly the honeymoon phase, so take this opportunity (of focus and positive energy) to schedule out the entire project with all decision-makers by having an extensive intake meeting to gather as much information about the family as possible, and generally educate and onboard your new clients as collaborators.

From the moment you are hired, you need to be communicating with your client. We use standing weekly emails starting on that very first Friday following the onboarding meeting. That schedule sets expectations and communication parameters right from the start.

Two weeks prior to the next collaboration, which is the Conceptual Design Meeting (CDM), we collect the balance of the flat design fee. If we don't have that payment, we remind our client that it is due prior to the first presentation, as our work is intellectual capital in nature at this point, so no developed designs will be disclosed without full payment. Our clients completely understand this condition because we laid out this timeline and expectation from the very first interaction. And our client is happy to pay the balance, as they are excited to see our design for their home. Their payment triggers confirmation of the upcoming presentation.

Do you see how I'm positioning payments to kick off positive actions by my firm? This approach is key to happy clients and a completely empty accounts receivable report. When your process is clear, efficient, and repeatable, you have more time to do what you do best: design.

At the CDM, we review the layout, a key elevation, aesthetic direction with mood boards and high-level samples, as well as the actual furnishings investment estimate. Our clients love this meeting! We give them plenty of information to understand the design direction, while still allowing the FIE to be flexible and open to their input.

We include one round of revisions at this time. We ask that any revisions are given to us together (not in dribs and drabs) and within one week of the CDM. Unless we are drastically changing the scope, we are able to incorporate those edits into our scheduled follow-up meeting within two weeks. Remember, we established the project schedule at the very beginning, giving a natural sense of urgency to "stay on schedule."

In the past, I resisted telling clients how long design and execution actually take, but I learned my lesson. Now, I use that up-front message to my advantage. I tell them the overall schedule in client onboarding. They inevitably groan and ask for it to go faster. I tell them where they can speed things up: Timely decisions at the two times allowed in the contract for edits. In other words, get any changes in to me within one week and stick to scheduled meetings and we'll stay on track, So, instead of being a constant disappointment to clients when a project drags and drags, the timeline also gives me internal deadlines that I can plan for. I never wonder what I should work on next, as each project is pipelined internally to dovetail with the meeting schedules.

Upon the client's approval of the design layout, FIE, and the aesthetic direction, we move on to the Detailed Design Phase. Here, we nail down each and every detail and every related cost, making sure that they always tie back to what we agreed on in the Conceptual Design Phase.

The purpose of the Detailed Design Meeting (DDM) is to review the entire project, each detail, fabric, finish, and all of the associated proposals. Again, the client is welcome to give us one round of revisions, all at the same time, and within one week of the meeting to stay on schedule. At this stage, our clients cannot wait to have this design come to life, and are happy to pay 100 percent up front (plus freight and tax) and 50 percent for labor to get this project in action. Furthermore, they are so happy that they hired a designer to handle purchasing, execution, and installation.

Onto the Execution Phase!

Let's be honest, the Execution Phase is hard. *This phase is the number-one best reason to stop charging hourly.* Sending an invoice to someone when you've already taken payment for 100 percent of the furnishings and trashed their house is not recommended. They are exhausted by the expense, the dust, and the lengthy timelines. With a fee-based project structure, at least you can ease up on the invoicing at this point.

One very valuable thing we do—and I highly recommend that you start doing it right now if you don't already—is sending an email to clients every Friday with a complete update of where the project stands. Status updates, schedule updates, upcoming meetings, open proposals with a link to approve and pay. That regular connection keeps the lines of communication open in between those times where you may not have meetings scheduled and *consolidates* communication. So instead of emailing them every time we have a question or a detail to convey—provided their response is not time-sensitive—we simply add it to the weekly email draft. Believe me, in a world of email overload, that tactic helps us get each email to them read every week.

Finally, installation begins, and our clients can see the light at the end of the tunnel. There's hope! Take advantage of that uptick in emotions—it's time to send the final labor invoice. The wording in our agreement states that labor balances are due two weeks prior to scheduled completion. That stipulation means that you should collect the final payment *prior* to getting to the punch list phase of a project. You know this step is crucial if you've ever had *that* client. If you haven't, thank your lucky stars and take my word for it.

If you meet resistance to the final labor bill, gently remind your client that you only work with trades of the highest integrity and that you are committed to your client and to their project until they are completely satisfied. If they still stall, remind them that in this day and age of internet reviews, all the leverage that they might need to get everything completed satisfactorily is under their control. You also can mention that you need time to process payment on your end and subsequently pay the hardworking trades that will have completed the beautiful job. I find that my clients are fine with this structure, again because I point it out very clearly from the very beginning.

Would I stop a job to wait on payment? You bet I would (and have). Contract work is a pay-to-play business. I do charity work elsewhere.

But I usually hold off until the final meeting about the turnkey project you are delivering so that the client sees the entire vision coming together over those final few days. Clients often are flabbergasted that their home could look so good, and they're ready to pay that labor bill. No further invoice becomes the icing on the cake. Imagine saying, "Nope, we're square," as you kindly fluff the last pillow and take your obvious victory lap toward their referral to friends and associates!

The "meeting then payment" structure is strategic: Have payment induce action. We put the ball in our client's court to move on to the next phase. The whole system clarifies the delicate balance between client and designer.

The investment that clients want to make in their home, that's theirs. The aesthetic design direction? We'll figure out that aspect together. The flat design fee and business structure, that's mine. Clarifying all of the details up front, from the very first contact, gives clients and designers clear lanes in which to stay. That certainty, combined with sensitive timing, has changed my business completely.

The End Game

We are clear at the beginning about whether or not we fit into a client's investment estimate and timeline. Because we are clear and totally up front with those realities, we don't always get the job, but surprise desertions are avoided. With a successful presentation and contract in hand, we then provide top-notch service all the way through—exactly the same A+ service to each and every client, each and every time.

Furthermore, the process works throughout the entire project. We maintain the flat fee, timeline, and process. Yet we completely empower the client to set their investment budget after we create an investment estimate of the desired scope. We also engage the client to move on to the next phase via approval and payment. After they pay the design fee, they again are in the driver's seat on how much they want to spend. We then outline a project timeline, but once more, they are in the driver's seat to make decisions and provide payment. *Their* action is what moves the project forward. We don't need to chase them, and because we set timelines and investment estimates that are completely attainable and realistic, we are calm, cool, and collected.

It wasn't always that way, however! I used to tell my husband that I needed to "pull an all-nighter" (which, when you are a working mother, means staying up past 1:00 a.m.). His response frustrated me to no end, "Why? If you are that busy, you need to raise rates and extend timelines to work for your schedule." At the time, I railed and raged at his non-entrepreneurial response. What did he know about running a small business? He's a "corporate man...." Turns out, I raised rates and now communicate timelines that work for me! I do not take on whatever timeline the client proposes or demands, and am sleeping like a baby.

Work smarter, not harder. Systematize the work, and then work the system. Do not deviate. Every single time that I deviate from our calculated and clarified plan, it shows me, once again, that those systems are in place for our joy and profitability. I want both. If I sacrifice either of those, I no longer want to be involved in the project.

Additional Reinforcement

Do you know other ways to set client expectations upfront (instead of reacting when the project goes off the rails)?

I cannot recommend enough the need to have Frequently Asked Questions (FAQs) on your website or as a handout. Check out mine. They are right to the point and a great place to prescript those tough topics (like paying 100 percent up front or your refund policy on custom furnishings). Set them up so that you aren't reacting to a client; rather refer them to your stated company policy.

In addition to FAQs, also address your timeline, structure, payment terms, all of it, in your design agreement and your design agreement presentation. Even if you are a one-person firm, you are one astute human, backed by policies.

Discuss the emotional timeline of a design project. Talking about that dark and dangerous place before going there (when you've taken a chunk of their money and trashed their house) is incredible. Later, when tension or impatience threatens, you can make a charming reference to the chart and the rise from the ashes to come. Ask that they stick with you and see this thing through, because hesitancy is a natural feeling at certain times during the project, but remind them that it's going to be amazing soon.

Stand in Your Space

It's *your* business. Make sure you love it and how it's working for you.

Stand in your space. If something is bringing you angst, stress, or is not profitable, it's time to change those results. Your business does not need to and should not be one-sided. Set it up for joy *and* profit. You can have a business that brings you both.

Your success means that you have to have happy clients. They need to be so thrilled, in fact, that they rave about you and tell all their friends and associates how great you are—how joyful and professional and beautiful working with you is.

*This is your **"Where did I drop the ball?"** moment.*

Are there areas where you consistently get pushback? Where the same problem arises, over and over, only with different clients? We can always trace a problem back to that one moment when we could have changed the outcome. The hard part is facing it because we so desperately want to cling to, "It wasn't my fault."

I remember the look in Sandra's eye when I said that truth to her. I could see it hit her like a stomach punch, and I felt just horrible for her. She was so truly distraught at the collapse of yet another project that she didn't see that the ball was in her court. Because she thought the problem was happening **to her**, she hadn't considered it was happening **because of her**. But when you look at it with new eyes, as Sandra did, you learn that you can reframe the conversations going forward, you can implement new processes going forward, you can course-correct and create a positive outcome for yourself and for your clients going forward. What an amazing feeling to step into! And as evidenced by Sandra's subsequent, undeniable transformation and success, you can see that extraordinary results are attainable.

Hard work? No question.

Worthwhile work? Most definitely.

So, what will you tackle now?

Start with that look in the mirror, next find the whisper of your inner voice, then seek help and advice. Remember to include the vision of your **dream** business and take that last step, take decisive action.

I hope Sandra has inspired and empowered you to believe that you can face obstacles head on. With intention and hard work it is possible to create a business that is a place of joy and profit.

-LN

About the Author

Sandra Funk is the CEO and principal designer of House of Funk, a greater New York area design firm working wherever great clients need us. This is interior design with a soul and a sense of place; reflecting your desires, personality, and style. House of Funk creates thoughtful homes with an emphasis on clean lines and soulful touches, all rooted in tradition. Sandra is an accredited professional for the Sustainable Furnishings Council. Sandra's award-winning design work has been featured in publications such as *Elle Decor, House Beautiful, The Huffington Post, Apartment Therapy, Aspire Design & Home,* and *Luxe Interiors + Design.* With almost two decades in the interior design industry, Sandra launched the Interior Design Standard in the spring of 2020, a template for designers to utilize her streamlined processes and business structure to bring joy and profit to their own design business.

Sandra Funk has been a featured guest on *A Well-Designed Business®* podcast episodes 3, 145, and 520.

CHAPTER 2

Sara Lynn Brennan

As you read Sara's chapter, notice how she describes herself: "I have an extreme amount of drive and enough grit to do anything I put my mind to." In my experience, it is not uncommon for many of us to overestimate how we show up in the world. We imagine we are doing more than we are, but Sara is right on point. Over the last several years, I have watched her show up and do the work with the exact drive and grit she has described.

Why am I specifically drawing your attention to this commitment? Because documenting every system and process in your business is a Herculean task. The sooner you realize this, the easier it will be to get to the work. In my first book, **The Making of A Well-Designed Business®,*** I talked about how we all are looking for that magic pill. We want the magic that unlocks the mysteries of a profitable business. I said it then and I will say it again: You are the magic pill. You have to do the work. Like Sara, you have to have drive and grit, and you have to do more than just show up.

Follow Sara's advice. Reflect on your business and the processes you have in place and the ones that are missing. Make a list of every area you need to address and then commit to doing the hard work. When you do, the benefits earned will affect all aspects of your business. By far the most valuable benefit is your growth as a confident, capable business owner. When you know you know what you are doing, then you truly own your role as the CEO of your business. That knowledge is the magic pill. This transformation results in attracting, securing, and expertly managing your ideal projects. The kind of projects that bring you happiness and profitability.

-LN

Showing Up Is Not Enough

Sara Lynn Brennan

If you want to be successful, you have to have a plan. It's as simple as that. You can't show up without a plan and say, "Hey, I'm a designer." Heck, you can't even go on vacation or go to the gym without a plan. Arriving at your destination is just the beginning; it's what you do after you get there that makes all the difference.

Have you ever thought about life like that? Almost everything we do can be calculated with a plan, process, or system. LuAnn and I talked about that reality during one of our podcast episodes. You might recall this conversation, which went something like this: I called LuAnn one summer morning during my first year in business and said to her, "I don't get it. I have my 10-step process, but I still feel like I don't have any control of my projects, the clients are running the show, and things are not going well. What the heck am I doing wrong?" LuAnn asked me what kind of subprocesses each of my 10 steps had, like how they were documented, and how my assistant and I tracked them. And that's when I got silent. "Crap! Are you telling me I need a process for each step of my process?" Having to answer "yes" to her reply felt impossible and, frankly, unnecessary for someone like me, when at the time I was a #babydesigner (LuAnn's term for someone who is just starting their journey as a designer) through and through. Why would I need to document all of that stuff...when it was primarily just my design assistant and me? What's the point of all the documentation? I didn't like it, I didn't get it, and I most certainly didn't want to do it! Stage one always is denial.

During our call, however, I had the "aha" moment. Honestly, that "aha" changed my business. In that moment, I realized it's not the documentation that is of such value, it's the exercise of

27

creating the documents. It's the plan...it's the process!

From then on, I literally saw everything differently. I realized every successful business is a big process with subprocesses throughout. The perfect example of it is something that LuAnn and I have talked about before—the "lawn mower" example. Let's say you are hiring someone to mow your lawn for you. You don't simply say "have at it" without first discussing costs, frequency, and process. You want answers. Will the guy bring his own mower or use yours? Who provides the gas? What pattern should they mow it in? What does he do with the clippings? How much does it cost, and how frequently will he mow? All of those decisions are made *prior* to his showing up. Can you imagine how that engagement might go without a plan? The yard could be full of jagged zigzags, clippings everywhere, he ran out of gas, and the cost was three times more than you thought. On the other hand, with a plan, the relationship could be exactly what you were hoping for. You see, you've planned so that the guy can't just show up and do whatever he wants. You can't just show up either. You need a plan in place to achieve your desired outcome, whatever that may be.

So, let's think about that analogy in terms of your current situation. You decided to open a design business. You probably created a logo, an Instagram or Facebook account, and maybe even a business website. Now what? You showed up and said, "Hello, world. I'm your designer!" But what's next? Let's be real for a second. Who cares that you're there? Why should they care? Who are you? What do you stand for? Showing up with your designer hat on is lovely, but what perspective do you have to offer? What do you believe in? How will you manage your projects? How can you be certain that you will not lose time, energy, and money in building this thing? How can you find the clarity to create the design firm that you deserve and dream of? The world needs you, I'm certain of it, but you need an action plan *before* you show up. And that's where I can help!

Three Actions to Explode Your Design Business

In the remainder of this chapter, I am going to outline three very actionable steps that will help you show up, kick butt, and take names, but you have to be willing to take this journey seriously. You should probably know, I'm not your typical coach, boss, or colleague. I like to talk things out, share experiences, and offer straightforward advice. I don't use typical business buzzwords that we all know, but can't really relate to. I share advice based on my experiences and emotions as a designer, educator, and interactive coach—a rare combination in our industry. I've suffered through much of what you're going through; in fact, I'm in the trenches with you right now as I'm building my own business from the ground up. But I've found ways to succeed at a rapid pace, and I want the same for you, which is why I'm willing to share my strategy to help you build the dream design business that you want.

Action 1: Craft Your Cause

Where are you going with this whole design thing? That question sounds kind of crazy, doesn't it? But when you decided that you wanted to open your design business, what was your intention? Are you looking for more of a hobby approach, do you want to be a force to be reckoned with in the design world, or something in between? At this point, some may suggest that you write out your "Mission Statement," which is all well and good, but if it's too formal or fancy for you to say to yourself regularly or when you are faced with a predicament, then it won't work. You almost have to back into that mindset and do what I call "Craft Your Cause" by thinking about *why* you are doing what you are doing. In essence, the real question is "What is your primary purpose for getting up and grinding it each and every day?" Make note of that purpose, and then ask yourself "why" with each answer to keep digging deeper until you have your *real* answer.

In creating your cause, it can be a list, paragraph, statement, or whatever you want it to be. The point is that you drill down into the real reasons for opening a design business. Throughout your journey as the business owner, you will use this "cause" as your compass, your north star, your guiding light as you are faced with opportunities or trials. I do think that your cause does eventually evolve into your client-facing mission statement. However, I think the wording of your actual cause is more personal and emotional. The words that you choose are ones that evoke grit and drive when you need it. Your cause will also help you identify what is sacred to you as a person; only you will know its meaning, but you will most likely build your company's core values around those ideas, so make your cause easily known to yourself. You may want to write it on a sticky note and keep it next to your desk to always remind you where everything stemmed from. Maybe you share it with your employees, maybe you don't. What you do with it in that context doesn't matter. The point is that you know who you are, what you're doing, and why you're doing it.

Your cause will be especially helpful as you become more successful and encounter more and more opportunities. For example, if you initially created your design firm to be a good example and role model for your children, but you get and take on so many projects that you are being pulled away from your family more and more, then your cause probably does not align with your action. Sometimes that result is a hard realization to have, but it's these gut checks that will keep you on the straight path toward your goals in the long run.

For me, I struggled with that insight for a while early on. I was getting advice from a lot of people about what I should do with my business, and I got in my own way. I had some self-doubt and was battling with the real reasons that I wanted to be a designer in the first place. I was lacking clarity in where I was going, who I was serving, and how my business "worked." It wasn't until I got fed up with a few projects, clients, and myself that I decided I was either going to quit or get clear on my goals. And the truth is that early on, my business was losing money and pulling me away from my family. I was a mess about all of it, and it sucked. When I realized that I didn't really have goals, despite all of my efforts, I got real with my business and myself: something had to change.

Following that revelation, I sat down with myself and dug deep into why I decided to open a business in the first place. It wasn't for personal validation, although sometimes I did feel like I had something to prove to the world or myself. I remembered that I decided to open a business so that I could contribute financially to my family's bottom line with the goal of earning enough money to pay off our pretty significant mortgage within the first five years of owning my company.

During my first year of business, though, the mess that I was in wasn't propelling me toward my goal. Quite the opposite: It was killing me, and my family was suffering because of it. No thank you! From that point on, I "Crafted My Cause" and identified what success looked like for me. I vowed to only take on projects within the aesthetic that felt authentic to me in order to help me establish a niche in which I absolutely knew I could succeed. I was going to stop talking about being "new" to the industry and to start showing clients that I was the real deal. I met with a finance coach and crafted a clear strategy to meet my income goals. I created unique design offerings that I now call "my packages," which displayed my clear process, expectations, and deliverables for my clients. No more "discounts," no more resentment, and no more nonsense. I started to get really clear about where I *didn't* want to go, which lead me to where I wanted to be—a family supporter with a six-figure salary in my second year of business. Do you see the power of hitting rock bottom and finding clarity? I sure do!

Action 2: Build It, Babe

Now that you have "Crafted *Your* Cause" and identified why you decided to start this business, you need to get to work on building out your actual business branding, processes, and services. Maybe you're just starting out, or maybe you hit the ground running 10 years ago and it's time for a reset. Whatever the case, I recommend you invest money and time into your logo, website, photography, and processes. Buy the best services you can afford at the time. If you want luxury clients, you will need to reflect that level in your branding. We attract what we post to Instagram, Facebook, or our website (in our very visual industry), so it's important that we look the part. That appearance applies to the "Services" tab on our website as well. If clients cannot clearly visualize what it would be like to work with you, why would they bother to inquire?

You will find a lot of clarity when you go through the exercise of writing out your design services or ("packages") on your website. It will force you to articulate what you do and how your processes will work, which will provide both you and the client with the clarity needed to proceed and take the next step.

That work is not the last task you need to complete, however.

The biggest "build" in which you will most likely have a heavy hand is the crafting of your internal and client-facing processes. I seriously recommend that you do not design for anyone until you have thought through how you will get them done. I also actually recommend that you don't even take a "Discovery Call" (a new client phone call) until you have a plan. It's not that I think you can't juggle all the tasks at once. I'm sure that you can. I just know that you would be more confident about your abilities if you had a great process in place. I know it because I've dropped the ball several times myself, even when I thought I was a good juggler. It turns out that I was overconfident in my multitasking and winging-it skills, which led to a lot of pain, agony, and the realization that I needed something more concrete to keep me on track.

As small business owners, our reputation is everything. If we get one bad review for one stupid mistake that we made, our clients can make it known to the world very quickly and easily. It's not worth the risk to operate your business without processes because you *will* mess up. So, let's look at the type of established processes needed to get you up and going with confidence so that you know how they will run from start to finish. I'll walk you through the way to build out your processes. I'll outline the steps, and you take it from there. With the bones and structure provided, you will have just what you need to get your process and systems in place.

Build Your Design Processes

(1)   Discovery Phase

In this phase, you will identify how you will answer inquiries as well as how to create a process for each. For example, what is the exact procedure in your firm when someone messages you on Instagram, emails you, or calls you? How do you respond? Do you capture their information in a database? What is the next step? Is it the same process every time? Do you send a follow-up email? You may know all of these answers and steps, but have you documented them? If you hired someone tomorrow, could they execute the process precisely, the same way every time, without asking you constant questions? If the answer isn't a loud and resounding "yes!" then you have some process work to do.

You also want to think about the ultimate goal of each phase you are in. In the Discovery Phase, the goal is to turn each inquiry into a paid consultation or service. So, how will you ensure that outcome happens? Write out email templates and scripted conversations to create a repeatable process to nurture and guide your potential client through your cycle and close them with a sale. If you can ensure that each client who goes through your intake process has the same wonderful experience, you will see more sales conversions while also building out a strong reputation for yourself.

I recommend that you don't go past this phase of the design process until you are ready. Stopping at this point may not be possible for some because you are already up and going with clients, but I recommend you nail down your Discovery Phase as soon as possible so that you can potentially delegate or automate some of this work though a Customer Relationship Management (CRM) software tool. All of my intake process is essentially scripted and automated, and it's amazing! I wake up some mornings to find that someone has booked a call or a consult with me, and I didn't have to put in effort to make that happen! This happens only because I have a very specific system and process in place.

If you start creating processes for your Discovery Phase but don't feel you are ready to move on to full service or other level(s) of design, don't worry. You can make a very nice living by doing multiple design consultations each week, and operating that way carries no shame. The idea is that you don't bite off more than you can chew until you're ready for it, and when you have a plan or a process for each service that you offer, you can take on the next level.

(2)   Design Phase

Ideally, before you ever start designing, I want you to think about the various types of design services that you will offer. I'm not necessarily talking about your consultations, but more along the lines of full-service, e-design, or DIY design services. I recommend that you nail down exactly what you want to offer to clients and write out a very clear process for each offering. Start with the service that you believe will be your "bread and butter," and build that process out first. The reward for this hard work is once you have a core process nailed down, you can adapt that one process to create others.

For the best results, I recommend that you create two document versions, one for a client-facing process and another for your internal process. You will share the client facing process, which is your high-level version, with your clients as a roadmap for them to refer to throughout the design process to help you manage and set their expectations. On the roadmap, you can also set dates for your milestone meetings early on to avoid any scheduling conflicts with your clients. Alternately, your internal design process document should completely outline every single process and subprocess, ensuring tasks get done, crosschecked, and completed exactly how you want them to from start to finish. Your internal design process document is worth its weight in gold.

Your Design Phase processes will always be unique to you, your business, and your staff. It is also a fluid document that you should amend and update regularly, as you grow and evolve and perfect your business and its systems. Once you are confident in your processes, I highly recommend you input them into a workflow database, such as Asana, Trello, or Basecamp, where you can assign tasks and roles throughout your team. The more you can document and check along the way, the smoother your projects will go.

(3) Procurement/Build Phase

These last two phases will be very specific about how you run your individual business, so I will offer my insight and advice in crafting the processes.

During the Procurement/Build Phase, you will work alongside your partners, trades, and vendors to create processes and execute your project. The more people that you involve in your process, the more organized you need to be. Create a system for getting information to and from your contractors, window-treatment professionals, furniture vendors, receivers, etc., in a timely and efficient way. Always go the extra mile to communicate detail, and do what you can to bring clarity, not confusion, to the project.

(4) Completion Phase

When you get to the end of a design project, emotions are usually running high. Clients (and designers) are often nervous, excited, and probably a little tired. You especially want a process that ensures a smooth and very positive experience all the way through to the end. Write processes for how you want to prepare and execute your install, how and where you will shop for your accessories, if you will hire a professional photographer, and what you expect from the clients as you wrap up their project. I like to be sure that the final visits with my client are positive and that I am not asking for money in my last email or meeting.

Lastly, create a process to evaluate the success of the project with your client and your design team. This feedback will help you make adjustments to your processes that will positively impact future jobs.

Once you've taken the time to map out the phases listed above, you are ready to post your services on your website and social media outlets, talk about them with your clients, show up, and sell them.

Action 3: Show Up and Sell

You've done the work, and you are ready to show up. The "event" could be a networking meeting, a client consultation, a designer conference, etc., but the point is that because you have gotten really clear on your cause, services, and process, you can now be confident in your ability to be successful. You've done so much to lay the groundwork for your business, but you can't just shove it all into a folder and hand it to someone you meet. You must have a plan for how you are going to tell your story and win the attention of your clients and colleagues.

The best way that I've learned to sell is through stories. Sharing what you know and believe as well as how your knowledge and belief arose is an incredibly effective strategy in convincing clients to work with you *and* for people to understand who you really are. I'm not the first to come up with this concept; however, I can attest to the fact that it works. Like many of you, I hated selling, and I cringed at the thought of telling people what I do, let alone sharing with them why I'm so wonderful. But with some practice, confidence, and a mind shift, I was able to totally transform the way that I thought about sales and the benefits of it through stories.

Storytelling is pretty easy when you think about it—it's a pretty natural thing that people do. When the time comes to do it for your design business, you've already done so much of the legwork to craft a beautiful story. All you need to do is tell it. You've soul-searched and identified your "cause," and you've taken the time to outline your services and processes. Now you just need to talk about them. Explain to people why, deep down in your core, you believe in the power of interior design and how you have seen the way that you have been able to transform people's lives with your skill. Your stories and experiences will weave together to become an exciting narrative that is unique and authentic to you. You'll start to feel more and more comfortable speaking about the positive design experiences you've had, primarily because they will be based on facts and true stories that you really believe in. I don't know if you know this, but people don't really buy what you "sell." They buy into what you *believe*. If you can share proof through a real-life story that you truly believe in what you're selling, you're well on your way to success!

I'll give you a simple example to show you what I mean. Nobody can argue against the idea that 2 + 2 = 4. It's an actual fact. Try to tell a story about it. I bet that it's easy for you to do. Two apples fell from a tree, then two more fell, and all of the sudden we had four apples on the ground. I could keep going about what made the apples fall, what the weather was like that day, what kind of apples they were, or what we did with them, but I took a basic fact and made it into a narrative. That translation is what you are going to do with your business, but your story is going to be much better and more interesting than my apple example. I'm sure of it.

Here's a few storytelling exercises: Prepare three to four stories based mostly or entirely on fact about what you do, experiences you've had, and why you believe in what you do. Just like we would prepare our responses for an interview, you need to prepare a few stories that can be used to conform to any question that you might be asked about your business. At a consultation, for example, you know the client will ask you questions such as "How long does your design process take? How much does it cost? Can you explain what services you offer?" Anticipating such questions should be no surprise to you as the designer because you wrote out your processes. So, to answer, you simply go into a story about your recent project that is similar to theirs. The story starts, "The timeline from start to finish was about 12 weeks, and the investment was $X, and, Oh, my goodness! That project was beautiful! Let me show you a photo! You are just going to *love* what we did in that space." Perhaps you continue, "I see that you love antiques, and we found this amazing..." And there is your story. You answered the client's question with facts and continued to include the fairytale ending. If we have strong, preplanned scripts that become our go-to responses, then we start telling a factual story that doesn't feel like selling at all, but works—and works well.

So, there you have it. Master the three actions that I outlined, and you are ready to show up to whatever arena you want and own it. Do the preparation, search your soul, get real with yourself, put in the extra hours, find confidence, write out those processes, and believe that you can *sell* your expertise. If you don't believe that you can, nobody else will. When I decided to change my narrative, get clear on my cause, and show up as the confident boss lady I wanted to be, I started telling my story the way I wanted *others* to tell it. I built my reputation myself, from the ground up because I wanted to, and I had a very clear goal.

I am not a superhero, and I don't have a leg up on you. I do have an extreme amount of drive and enough grit to accomplish anything I set my mind to. Do you? How bad do you want it? Are you going to phone it in or *really* show up? The awesome result is that you will know when you've arrived at your destination with the preparation and clarity necessary to achieve the success for which you are looking. You'll feel it. You'll own it. You'll see it pay off. And you'll love it. Now, put yourself out there and practice as often as you can, get in front of clients, colleagues, tell your stories, and run with the big dogs because now you have a plan and absolutely know how to be successful.

Go, prepare, plan, *show up*, and be excellent!

That was the "why." Now, you are likely asking, "what about the 'how?'" This sounds impossible, and you're thinking, "tell me how I get this done in my business." There is no escaping it: the "how" is every bit as tedious and time-consuming as you imagine it to be.

Sorry.

Remember drive and grit? The "how" is where you will need them in spades. Here are a couple of tactics to get you started:

1.   Listen to Sara's podcast, episode #463. Sara explained her highlighter method for documenting her systems and processes. For weeks and months, she filled notebooks with every idea related to her design phases. On plane rides, in the middle of the night, after leaving a client or a vendor, and every time she thought "This is how I do this," or more importantly, "This is how I should have done that," she recorded it. Then, when she was ready to document her processes, she combed through everything she had written in her notebooks and color-coded the mountains of information.

- Discovery Process: *yellow highlighter*
- Design Phase: *pink highlighter*
- Procurement Phase: *orange highlighter*
- Reveal Install: *blue highlighter*
- Project Autopsy
- Post-Project Marketing Funnel

How brilliant is this? We all have lists and lists and notebooks full of the improvements we want to make to our business. Now pages of unorganized, random thoughts can be categorized so that you can actually create your detailed operations manual. Imagine—the way you do everything in your business, captured clear, concise, and documented.

2.   Next is to translate those notebooks, filled with ideas into your SOPs: Standard Operating Procedures. I will share what always works for me. I sit and begin by thinking very specifically, with a microscopic view of a particular task. Notice I said task, not project. Look for the tiniest of tasks within the steps of greater processes.

For example, what is the process for ordering a sofa? With our microscopic view, let's begin with the task of ordering only the fabric for a sofa.

- *Who specifies the pattern info?*
- *Where is this information found?*
- *How many yards do you need?*
- *Is the same fabric specified for different products going to different workrooms?*
- *How do you order it? Email, phone, fax?*
- *How do you pay for it? Proforma? 30-day terms? By check or credit card?*
- *Do you need a CFA (cutting for approval)?*
- *What do you do with the CFA?*
- *Where do you ship the fabric?*
- *How do I show that I have completed all these steps?*

We already have 10 steps, and we haven't yet addressed the sofa's actual style. Is there a skirt; is it tailored; how many pleats; what is the arm style; is there trim; nail heads; what about the filling? To order a sofa properly, the list needs to be specific and precise. This is the level of documented details you need for every single subprocess of every step in your business. It is the only way to ensure critical details are not overlooked or forgotten. It is also critical for scaling both your projects and your business.

You know what I always say: if you do not have a duplicable system for everything you do, you have a "you," not a business.

To get this documentation accomplished, start with one tiny task. Commit to do another one every day, or block a day a week, or a week a month. Do whatever it takes to get it done.

Drive and grit, drive and grit.

–LN

About the Author

Sara is an entrepreneur, CEO, and principal interior designer at Sara Lynn Brennan Interiors. Sara has become the first and only full-service interior design firm in Waxhaw, North Carolina, who specializes in Transitional Designs, where she and her design-build team take spaces from bare bones to beautiful by utilizing her exclusive, approachable, and stress-free design process, transforming and renovating homes from start to finish.

Sara's design work has been nationally published six times in the last year including publications such as *Romantic Homes*, *Traditional Home*, *Window Fashion Vision*, and *Cottages and Bungalows*, who recently offered her a role as a monthly columnist. She's also been noticed as a rising star among colleagues in the design industry being invited as a guest on podcasts, as a panelist at High Point Market, and as a host and speaker at local design events and shows.

Sara Lynn Brennan has been a featured guest on *A Well-Designed Business*® podcast episodes 463, 514, and 524.

Section Two

Protecting Your Business

CHAPTER 3

Jamie Lieberman, Esq.

The first time I spoke with Jamie, I knew that I would love her. Her voice is both calm and full of energy, and somehow at the same time. Why did this speak to me? Well, I want a lawyer who embodies confidence, who projects stability, steadiness. As a creative, just like you, I also like to be around engaging people and those who don't take themselves too seriously. That description defines Jamie: Composed and reliable, yet impassioned and relatable. And that's why she is known as the least "lawyery" lawyer there is!

In her chapter, Jamie does exactly what she does in real life: She explains matters like a lawyer, and then she explains them like a person. I value that trait—that gift—about her. She understands that the legal stuff isn't our superpower. She calmly, happily answers the same question three and four times (uh, yes, personal experience—LOL) and each time without one iota of silent (or not-so-silent) judgment.

Why do I mention this? The word "lawyer" in Spanish is **abogado**, in French it's **avocat**, in Italian it's **avvocato**. Sensing my drift here? Your lawyer is supposed to be your advocate, and in order to be your advocate, there must be mutual trust, respect, and open communication. You have to be able to ask the silliest of questions and know that you will be heard and answered. I sincerely hope you never really need your lawyer other than for writing perfunctory contracts, but if you were to find yourself in real trouble, your lawyer must be able to communicate with you in a way that makes you confident that you will be protected and safe.

The importance of a clearly written, comprehensive contract cannot be overstated. In her chapter, Jamie outlines the major areas that should be covered in your contract. Please compare your contract to her list. If you don't have a contract for your design business, please don't tell me about it! But I'll grant immediate forgiveness if you go now to get one. Here are your choices: Contact Jamie to get it set up, or take her advice and her outline of contract points to your own lawyer. Stat.

-LN

Secrets of a Well-Designed Contract

Jamie Lieberman, Esq.

You made it to the legal chapter. I know that dealing with legal matters can sometimes feel overwhelming or scary and that the thought of reading about contracts might be right up there with having a root canal. You have my promise, though, that we are going to provide this information in an easy and accessible way so that you can walk away feeling more confident in your understanding of important contract terms.

In this chapter, we are going to discuss a few important provisions in a client services agreement, define those provisions, and illustrate their importance using real-world examples from my legal practice. (Note to reader: This chapter has been created solely to provide information. Although I am a practicing attorney, no attorney-client relationship is created through the information provided. I highly recommend speaking with an attorney that specializes in working with design professionals for legal advice specific to your business.) Now, on to the good stuff!

A *well-designed* (see what I did there?) contract is written to protect both parties. In this chapter, we are going to talk about the following terms that appear in most well-written agreements: (1) scope; (2) third-party vendor provisions; (3) payment terms; (4) photography/social media clauses; and (5) limitations of liability and damages. I will explain each term and then illustrate how it is used through a situation that one of my clients has experienced. For ease of illustration, I have created a hypothetical client named Sandy who gets herself into some sticky situations. Although Sandy is fictional, design professionals frequently encounter these real-world challenges.

At the end of the chapter, I also have provided my top 10 tips for dealing with conflict that I have learned through my work as a practicing attorney. I hope those tips assist you in your business in the event that a conflict arises.

Scope

Scope is one of the most important sections in a well-written contract. The scope, or the parameters of the services offered, defines the boundaries of the relationship between the parties. To that end, it is in both parties' best interest to be as detailed as possible in the agreement to define the scope of the engagement. Scope should include: (1) a description of the services provided, (2) the expected deliverables, (3) the timeline for completion, (4) permitted communications, including number of emails and phone calls, (5) number of meetings, (6) rounds of permitted feedback (or changes, depending on the project), and (7) how the parties will proceed if the client wants to change the scope after the agreement has been signed.

That list might seem a bit daunting, especially when you are starting out with a new client. You might be wondering, "What happens if we have not decided some of those details at the time that the client is ready to sign the agreement?" Have no fear. There is a fix. If most of the details of the agreement have been decided, not knowing the details of one aspect of scope should not prevent you from moving forward. For example, timeline is frequently a moving target in design projects. For any provision that is not set in stone, such as timeline, we recommend including a sentence that the unknown detail will "be determined under separate cover." That statement is fancy "legal speak" to mean that the parties will decide that detail through a different means, such as email, at a later date. But here's the trick: Do not forget to follow through and memorialize the open term *in writing*. That follow-up will save a lot of future headaches.

To illustrate the pitfalls of an agreement that did not have a well-defined scope, let's look in on Sandy, who has entered into an agreement to assist a client in redesigning their living room. Sandy provided a flat fee quote to provide a new design and furniture options. Sandy, unfortunately, did not include a provision that limited the number of options provided or set a boundary around communications. Sandy's client was very anxious to complete this project because she was throwing a party in two months and wanted to showcase her new living room. Sandy provided the client with a beautiful plan. And, of course, the client loved the design—except that the client didn't like any of the furniture options that Sandy had provided and instead asked for new choices. For the next two weeks, Sandy provided multiple rounds of furniture options, none of which were resonating with her client. Sandy found herself in an endless loop of providing proposal after proposal with no end in sight. Frustrated, Sandy finally terminated the agreement and offered to refund the client's money. Thankfully, the client recognized Sandy's hard work, and the parties found a compromise. At the conclusion of the project, though, the value of Sandy's work far exceeded the amount paid by the client.

In hindsight, it was easy to see that Sandy failed to set boundaries on the number of revisions and options that she would provide to the client in exchange for the quoted price. During the contract-drafting process, however, it is easy to forget that provision unless you have a placeholder for it. Creating a template for your statement of work that includes blank spaces for all of the potential details in your scope will allow you to remember all the details needed for future engagements. Furthermore, by always using a template with the standard clauses in place, you can easily insert or delete any particulars specific to a project.

Third-Party Vendor Provisions

At some point during a designer's career, the question of how you work with third-party vendors is bound to arise. Therefore, establishing a policy related to your relationship with third-party vendors is important. A third-party vendor is an individual or business whose services are needed to complete the project but cannot be performed by you or someone employed by you. It can be anyone from a handyman to a plumber, an electrician, or a wallpaper vendor.

For those designers without any licensing restraints (i.e., different states have different rules for working with third-party vendors), a few common scenarios for third-party vendor relationships are: (1) you can remove yourself from the relationship between your client and a third-party vendor; (2) you can coordinate the third-party vendor's work, but require your client to contract with the vendor directly; or (3) you can contract with the vendor on behalf of your client and agree to be responsible for the vendor's work.

When creating that policy, understanding and following those licensing restraints is important. Some states, for example, do not allow designers to contract directly with the vendor unless other conditions have been met. Always verify your local licensing rules to confirm that your policy complies with your state's laws.

Once you have determined and have set the policy that best suits your business, being transparent with your client about the level of your involvement in managing the vendor(s) that will work on the project becomes very important. Including a provision in your agreement so that your client knows your role in relation to the vendor(s) is recommended. Best practice is to include language limiting as much of your liability as possible related to the work product to be provided by your vendor(s). If you choose option (1) or (2), listed previously, including a "limitation of liability" clause is desirable to restrict your client's ability to involve you in a dispute resulting from a vendor's work. If you choose option (3), however, limiting your liability to your client is more challenging because the client will not have a direct relationship with the vendor and will likely look to you for resolution if an issue arises with a vendor's work. In that scenario, you still can protect yourself by entering into a separate agreement with any vendor. That agreement should include all the details of the project—scope, timeline, payment terms, etc.—as well as an insurance provision and an indemnification clause to protect you in the event that the vendor fails to complete the work or completes the work below reasonable standards of quality.

Here's a worse-case situation. Sandy recently worked with a client to remodel her kitchen. Typically, Sandy does not get involved with the vendors, but as a favor to this client—a friend of a friend—she agreed to coordinate with a plumber to install the kitchen sink. Sandy recommended the plumber, introduced him to the client, and made herself available to the plumber so that the work could be completed while her client was away on vacation. Sandy even paid the plumber a deposit that the client reimbursed, and the client agreed to pay the remaining balance directly to the plumber upon return from vacation. While the plumber was installing the sink, he accidentally installed it incorrectly, causing $5,000 in water damage. The client demanded that Sandy pay for the damage even though Sandy did not cause the damage.

In this case, Sandy's contract was silent about conditions regarding third-party vendors, although Sandy had verbally stated that she did not want to be held responsible. To attempt to ease the dilemma, Sandy called the plumber, but he blamed the client for the issue and stated that he would not pay for the damage. Sandy was stuck in the middle without any recourse against either party and ended up paying for half of the damage to keep her client happy. A formal agreement with the vendor and a short clause in her client services agreement would have saved Sandy the expense. If you haven't set a consistent policy for working with third-party vendors, an attorney can create multiple versions of an appropriate clause so that you can pick and choose the right version that works for each client and contract.

Terms of Payment

Your terms of payment are critically important because we all want to get paid! You work hard and deserve to have a seamless invoicing process with as few questions or disputes as possible. Few things are as stressful as being worried about receiving payment or a client who questions an invoice. The possible adverse scenarios can seem endless when drafting payment terms, and that part of a contract frequently is the one that my clients change the most depending on their client. Each design business is different, and payment terms are usually not "one size fits all." Designers can use an hourly rate, a flat fee, a project-based fee, or some hybrid of those options. If you are billing by the hour, clients typically ask for an estimate. If you provide estimates to clients, we recommend including language in the estimate and in your contract that gives you the flexibility to change the estimate during the course of the project, particularly if unforeseen issues arise. Specific language initially will help avoid disputes later.

Additionally, you have to decide when you want to be paid, whether you take deposits and if you provide deposit refunds. We also recommend including a provision that gives you the ability to cease work on the project in the event a client fails to make a timely payment as well as a clause that awards you attorney fees and costs associated with collection efforts, including those involved in having to file suit. Another smart provision is to add interest to payments past their due date, but be aware that interest is hard to collect absent a lawsuit. A critical part of your payment terms is to link each payment to the deliverable(s) listed in the scope of work. Full circle, right? There is a method to the madness! Linking your payments to deliverable(s) ensures that you have fully defined the scope and haven't left any holes like poor Sandy did.

Be aware that service providers frequently encounter issues relating to payment, and attorneys field frequent inquiries to assist clients in payment disputes. Having clear payment terms will limit some of the potential for disputes.

Here's another avoidable situation with one of Sandy's contracts, in which a client repeatedly missed important payment deadlines. Sandy followed up with her client, who promised that the proverbial check was in the mail. For months, Sandy continued to incur expenses believing that her client was going to pay. When she finally decided to stop the work, Sandy's client owed her about $25,000. Although Sandy had the proper mechanisms in her contract to cease the work sooner, she felt badly for her client and was scared to deliver the hard talk about payment and termination. Sandy fell into the trap between wanting to protect her business and appearing too tough. She had to learn the valuable lesson that no matter how great your contract is, you have to be willing to enforce its terms and have those tough conversations. You are worth it!

Photography/Social Media Clauses

Social media has so many advantages to a business owner. And what better way to showcase your beautiful work than to show examples of real projects from a client's home or business? The easiest way to avail yourself of such additional benefit *and* avoid conflict is to insert a clause in your agreement that allows your use of before-and-after photographs of each project. Such agreements contain a provision that grants the designer the right to take the photos and to use them for marketing, promotional, and editorial purposes, including website, social media channels, and portfolios. The provision also should include a section that agrees to maintain client confidentiality so that your client feels comfortable giving permission. Best practice is to give your client an opportunity to opt out and to respect those wishes if the client does not want the project to be photographed or shared.

Another sticky situation might arise if you employ an outside photographer to take the photos on your behalf. Many clients get very excited to see their homes looking so beautiful and want to share the images as well, but be sure you have permission from the photographer to share them. The *last* thing you want is having your client receive a "cease and desist" letter from your photographer for using those images without permission. Many photographers only grant a limited license to the designer to use the images and ask for an additional fee if the client wants to use them too.

A contract is only as good as its terms. On another project, Sandy worked with a high-profile client on a large commercial project that was a very big business opportunity for her. Sandy was so excited about the progress of the project that she shared a few stories on her Instagram account with some sneak peeks of the progress. The client had given Sandy permission to share, but wanted to approve the images before Sandy posted anything publicly. In her excitement, Sandy forgot that she had made this agreement, and her client saw the posts. Although Sandy was careful not to reveal her client's identity, the client was very angry that Sandy had not followed the protocol in the contract and withdrew the permission to use any images. Sandy did not have any leverage to negotiate because she had broken the client's trust—and a material provision of the agreement. Fortunately, the project ended on a positive note, but Sandy had to work extra hard to rebuild her client's trust.

Limitation of Liability

Two other helpful provisions are a limitation of liability clause, which sets a cap for the amount of damages, and a limitation of damages clause, which sets a limit on the type of damages a party can seek if there is a breach of contract. Not all states allow for limitations of liability and/or damages, however, so it is important to check your state's laws to see what is allowed. Also, to be enforceable, a limitation of liability clause must be reasonable. When drafting a limitation of liability clause, a designer should consider the potential risks that can occur relative to the transaction and carefully create wording to protect against those risks. Neither limitation of liability nor limitation of damages clauses absolve a breaching party of liability, but they create a boundary so that the parties know the breadth of damages available in the event of a conflict.

Through a limitation of liability clause, a designer can set a limit for damages in terms of the amounts that either party can recover. Typically, a contract will limit damages to amounts due under the agreement, an amount that is covered by insurance or some other amount that is equitable to the parties. It is important that the amount chosen is fair and won't be considered too small if ever brought before a court.

A limitation of liability clause helped Sandy when she was in a rough spot. She contracted with a client to choose new furnishings for a living room for a flat fee of $10,000. While the furnishings were being delivered, there was some damage to her client's living room because of an error on Sandy's part. The damage had the potential to be especially costly, and Sandy was understandably nervous. Thankfully, Sandy had included a liability clause in her agreement that limited potential damages to the amounts paid under the agreement, or $10,000. Because Sandy's contract included that clause, she had some leverage to negotiate with her client and was able to resolve the dispute out of court.

Limitation of Damages

Similarly, a limit on the type of damages that a party can seek against the other party should be included in the contract. The different types of damages include: (1) Compensatory—damages to compensate the wronged party for the actual loss or for what was not done but should have been; (2) Liquidated—damages agreed to in advance where the actual amount is difficult to ascertain so long as it is not unreasonably large; (3) Punitive—damages designed to punish a party (those typically are not available in breach of contract actions); (4) Incidental—costs of keeping any more damage from occurring, such as arranging for substitute goods; (5) Consequential—the foreseeable consequences of the breach; and (6) Nominal—set amount if the actual amount cannot be determined or if there are no actual damages. The purpose of the different types of damages is to make "whole" the wronged party under the contract. Not every type of damage is allowed under a contract or in each dispute. Take great care to ensure that the limitation of damages clause does not conflict with other provisions in the agreement and is relevant to the agreed-upon transactions in your services agreement.

Resolving Conflict

We've talked about many tips and tools to help you draft a contract that minimizes client conflict. Creating an easy-to-read agreement that avoids using *legalese* can be a good selling tool as well. Starting off your relationship with your client in a transparent and honest way helps position you for success. But even the best relationships can experience unforeseen conflict. What happens when you find yourself in a dispute with a client or a vendor?

I spent many years of my legal career as a litigator, dealing with some very aggressive and difficult attorneys. Through those experiences, I have created my top 10 tips that you can use when you have to tackle conflict, whether it is with a client or a vendor.

Tip No. 1: Take a breath. Have you ever opened your email and received a shockingly rude message? Or picked up the phone only to find you are on the receiving end of a particularly difficult conversation? The first, and most important step, is to take a breath. If you find your heart racing or your stomach turning, take a moment to breathe and calm your nerves. If you are on the phone, ask to return the call at a better time. It is a good practice to approach conflict with a calm attitude. It helps to ensure that you are acting on logic rather than on emotion. The instinct to respond to a nasty message is to respond with the same or greater level of anger or hurt, and that action is the surest way to escalate a conflict.

Tip No. 2: Get more information. You may not be able to respond adequately to the issue without obtaining more information. Often, an email can be a good way to begin because your message is easier to digest, to review, and to avoid misunderstandings. An email gives you time to formulate your thoughts and to ensure that you are being respectful, no matter how angry or upset you might be. When seeking more information, your goal should be to narrow the focus so that you can start to see a path to resolution. Always lead with a welcoming tone and respectful language. Remember tip No. 1, and take a breath before sending anything electronically or in writing.

Tip No. 3: Listen and ask questions. When faced with conflict, most people instinctively start to defend themselves before they gather all of the facts. You will have your opportunity to lay out your position, but it is far more effective to do so when you have heard the other party. Never assume you know why the other person is angry or upset, because the cause is often about an issue other than the one that you expected. Having accurate information about the true root cause of the conflict makes coming to a resolution easier.

Tip No. 4: Formulate the issues and assess each party's position. Once you have gathered your information, the issues in conflict and each party's position should become clear. I like to create a chart so that I can see how far apart the parties are on each issue. Then, start with those issues that are closer together so that you can dispose of them quickly, create goodwill, and set up the resolution for those issues where the parties are more at odds.

Tip No. 5: Stay firm on the lines that cannot be crossed. With any conflict, setting clear boundaries in all business dealings is important, especially those that result in major issues. That decision becomes very personal because each business owner will have certain rules that are nonstarters. If the conversation veers toward a boundary, stay confident in your unwavering stance that those issues are not up for negotiation. Lastly, do not allow fear of conflict to motivate you to cross those boundaries.

Tip No. 6: Always remain calm when speaking to the other person, no matter how angry or upset you might feel. Even in my worst moments when another attorney is screaming at me, I make it a point to remain even-keeled. In fact, the angrier someone gets, the quieter my voice becomes. It is very hard to scream at someone who is not screaming back, and a calm demeanor can serve to cut through the tension.

Tip No. 7: Talk to a trusted associate. We all need a gut check. Sometimes that unnecessarily rude email has some valid points that you may need to consider. An uninvolved third party can often give you the perspective you need to plan your next steps. An honest conversation with a friend or colleague can do wonders to help put the conflict into perspective. Always protect confidential information when you speak to someone outside of your organization and avoid bad-mouthing or venting. And remember, your associate has to be willing to tell you things you may not want to hear. So, choose wisely, and take the time to incorporate your associate's objective input into your response.

Tip No. 8: End conversations that become too aggressive. No matter how emotional the situation is or even if one party is in the wrong, no one deserves to be disrespected or spoken to in a demeaning or rude manner. If the other party curses or uses personal insults, I immediately stop the conversation and let them know it can be continued at a later date when they are calmer. I do this in a firm but respectful voice, and the behavior does not typically repeat itself.

Tip No. 9: Separate emotion from logic. It is hard for most people to admit when they are wrong. I get it. Lawyers are the worst about that! In order to resolve conflict, however, both parties typically need to make some concessions. To do that, you need to be able to logically consider which positions aren't as important to you so that you can focus on those that are.

Tip No. 10: Compromise. I know. Sometimes it just plain sucks to give in when you feel that you are right. But try to keep in mind that conflict takes your time, your energy and costs you money whether or not you are paying someone to fight that battle on your behalf. The amount of time you are taking to analyze the situation, talk to your friends and replay conversations in your head is time away from other valuable tasks in your business and your life. Conflict has an emotional aspect to it and requires energy that is frequently better expended in positive ways. That guidance doesn't imply that you should allow yourself to be taken advantage of by another party. Instead, use the logic discussed in the tips above and think about whether the conflict is worth the fight or if a simple, equitable compromise could resolve it.

Following the recommendations above and creating a framework to handle conflict will allow more control over the process when issues arise. Having a great contract also helps limit conflict in that the expectations of the parties are set ahead of time. Needless to say, it is much easier to negotiate at the beginning of a designer/client relationship than it is when an actual conflict arises. If you can anticipate the potential speed bumps during the design process and resolve them ahead of time in the contract, you can limit surprise developments and look forward to receiving happy client emails.

See what I mean? When Jamie speaks, she speaks to you—a designer, a real person. Every single professional with whom you do business should respect you enough to speak to you in a way that **you** *understand, not that* **they** *understand.*

How about your contract? Does it measure up to Jamie's points? I hope it does, but if it doesn't, please take action. In all the conversations that I have had with designers over the years, you cannot imagine the things that have gone wrong and have put a designer's business in jeopardy. One time, a designer with whom we were working had artfully designed custom tiles for a client's bathroom—very expensive, one of a kind—and after tremendous lead time, they were finally installed. Amazing, impressive, loved by the designer and the client alike. But wait—the plumber ran the hot water to the cold tap and ran the cold water to the hot tap! You know what happened next, right? The gorgeous tile had to come down, new tile had to be ordered, horrible delays ensued, time and money were wasted, and heartache galore for all involved. Fortunately, the designer's rock-solid contract ensured that this plumber didn't try to play the same game that Sandy's plumber played. Saved by the contract!

Finally, I'd like to stress the number one purpose of your contract is to prevent you from needing your contract! When you have an airtight contract that you have discussed with and had signed by your client and you find yourself with the threat of a serious conflict, you have the advantage. You will confidently remind your client: "Of course, I know you recall that we covered this in the contract, so why don't we see how we can resolve this?" When your client knows you are standing on firm ground, somehow issues get resolved a little bit more easily. However, if there is no contract or a flimsy contract at best, clients are more apt to dig in their heels and make demands. So, remember this: The first job of a well-crafted contract is to ensure that everyone works toward resolution **without pulling out the contract.** The second job of a well-crafted contract is to protect you like a bulletproof vest if calm heads leave the building and the parties aren't willing to come to agreement. In that case, your contract better be impenetrable. The goal is—the hope is—that you never need your contract, but you have to have it to not need it.

-LN

About the Author

Jamie, owner and founder of Hashtag Legal, has been a practicing lawyer for nearly 15 years. As an experienced entrepreneur, Jamie understands the unique needs of business owners at different stages in their organization's growth. Today, she partners with clients across verticals, including influencer marketing, creative services, and e-commerce. She has a deep commitment to making legal advice accessible and regularly speaks about legal matters, the art of negotiation, and entrepreneurial topics at leading industry events such as Alt Summit, Podcast Movement, and FinCon and as an expert source for media like *Digiday* and *Forbes.* You can also catch her as a cohost on *The FearLess Business* podcast.

Jamie Lieberman, Esq., has been a featured guest on A *Well-Designed Business*® podcast episodes 454 and 547.

CHAPTER 4

Kimberly Merlitti

Chief cook and bottle washer. We hear this often when describing an entrepreneur. It means you get to...well, it means you **have** to do anything and everything in your company.

In the beginning, this is especially true. Sometimes, it is true for more years than we would like it to be. Is it a good practice, though? No, not really. Especially if you have dreams of growing and scaling up. And it's especially inefficient when you are not good at every skill required to run a business.

An all-too-common mistake is skipping over or not paying enough attention to the areas we aren't strong in.

I get it. Been there, done that. (Um, full disclosure, been there, do that. We're all human.)

So, you've been busy, and you never quite learned how to understand your cash flow, your pipeline projections, and your—as The Vin Man says—cost to be open number.

Dealing with budgets, projections, invoicing, and finances in general are the top areas I see creatives avoid, evade, avert, elude... shirk, shun, sidestep...hmm, this wouldn't be you, would it?

If you don't know how to read your QuickBooks reports let alone know how to use them to manage and run your business, you keep sliding by, figuring it out as you go. Sometimes, it goes okay; sometimes, not so much. When I asked a listener who joined one of our LuAnn University courses why she invested in the class, she answered, "I feel like I've been building a car as I'm driving it 75 miles an hour down the road."

Amen. We all know this feeling.

Do you get that queasy feeling in your stomach when it's time to talk with your bookkeeper or your CPA? Are you already many months in business or—yikes—already many years in business? Do you think to yourself before every meeting, "What is she going to say? Is everything okay with my business?"

This ends today. Or at least, today is the beginning of the end of this.

–LN

Money Is Everything

Kimberly Merlitti

It was spring of 1998, and I was 28 years old. I had just decided not to pursue a career in law enforcement, and I applied for other jobs all around Portland, Oregon. I was raised in Portland. I was a Reserve Police Officer in Portland. I have ex-boyfriends in Portland. My family lives in Portland. Portland felt like a small town at this point in my life, so I was not scared; I was just worried about changing my mind about my profession. Law enforcement had always been my goal since watching *The Silence of the Lambs*, which came out in 1991.

I applied mostly to administrative jobs. Most of them were for office management work or supporting someone who was a professional in a particular industry. One day I got a call from the Office Manager at Swinerton Builders. The position was supporting a Project Manager. He was a lot of fun to work with, and he let me research things about the industry that I did not understand. The company was on a software system that was DOS-based. (For those who don't know what DOS means, don't worry. I still don't know exactly what DOS means. It's just an older type of programming software.) No problem, right? After studying criminal law and driving like a bat out of hell in a patrol car, learning a new software did not seem like a hard challenge.

You are probably wondering why I am taking the time to explain all of this. I am not one of those soft-spoken accountants—or quiet. Accounting is all about rules. I thrive on rules and structure. I was raised in a household where if we even got near drugs or alcohol, we were not allowed to play sports (in my case, soccer) or go out with our friends. If we wanted clothing or other items that were not in the household budget, we were expected to get a job, even if we were 12 years old. At the time, I thought all of those conditions were completely normal. I thought every household had those kind of rules. So, I never stepped out of line.

Rules remain important to me, but as I was learning the software program at Swinerton at that time, I did not realize that I was learning the rules of accounting.

In my first year at Swinerton, the company decided to convert to a Windows-based system for their accounting/project management software. The Chief Financial Officer (CFO) at the time asked if I wanted to make some overtime money and, of course, I answered yes. So, with new software and about six months later, they transferred me to the accounting department.

The company moved me to San Francisco in 2003 and gave me a title as a Staff Accountant, but I was more a problem solver. I quit that job due to boredom, and I was hired as an Accounting Manager at an architectural firm. Then five years after that, I was recruited into an interior design firm as the Accounting Manager. During all of those jobs, I was studying part time in the evenings to obtain my Masters in Accounting degree. Then, I made a decision that changed my life. I started my business. I will always remember the day that I opened my business bank account. I thought to myself, "No turning back now."

In the six years of school that it took me to get my Masters, not one professor taught the type of revenue structure that occurred in construction, architecture, or interior design. As I had worked in all those fields, I observed one major consistency that all the owners of those companies were addressing on a regular basis: Where was the next job coming from? How could they guarantee that they could make their payroll and rent every month if they did not know where the next job was coming from? In construction, they had this program called Suretrack, which would allow us to provide a schedule and budget for each job, but once I started interior design, I did not find a program like this. How was I going to track a schedule and budget on each job?

Grad school taught me all about the subject of cash-flow issues specifically and how to track revenue for manufacturing, service, and nonprofit companies. Years later, I thought to myself that type of work experience was irreplaceable, which made me grateful for what I had absorbed while working in the field of construction.

Then in 2005, I started working for an architectural company that had 25 employees. The pressure was on me during this period to project how long our revenue was going to fund our company. The seven partners depended on me to let them know they needed to bring in work. I also knew that the bigger the firm became, the more dependent we were on a healthy cash flow. When I left there in 2008, the firm employed over 100 people.

Each job that we took in had a schedule and a budget assigned to it. I took that information, entered it into a simple spreadsheet, and whenever I started to see a dip in the revenue to fund the company and make a profit, I would let the partners know. The whole idea of the spreadsheet was to find out in October that we needed work in February. Waiting until February to break this news to the owners would not do the company any good. Also, I would be out of a job! As it turned out, I did not need some fancy software to determine when we needed new projects. But I did need a schedule and a budget.

Another five years later and I started in interior design accounting. Nearly all of the jobs were residential, and I was shocked to find out that work was being started without a schedule or a budget in most cases. So, of course, my first question was,

"How do you know when the money will run out?" No one could answer my question. I provided the answer: I started working with the owner of each interior design firm to determine the schedule for each of their current jobs and put that information into a spreadsheet. I had to teach my interior designers to attach a schedule and budget to each of their jobs if there was any hope of my helping those businesses to project their cash flow.

"Is there any way you can guarantee how much money you will take in six months from now? How about three months from now?" In my seven years in construction accounting and five years in architectural accounting, I was asked that exact question multiple times. My answer was (and is) that accountants can never guarantee anything, but we can plan the shit out of it.

Cash-Flow Projections

There are two common variables—schedule and budget—that I need in order to keep track of cash-flow information, but in my experience those details are missing most frequently. Since the number one worry and question from clients that I get as a CFO is, "Will I have enough money to keep my business running in six months?" I'm immediately thinking to myself, "How can you not have a schedule and budget for your jobs?" I can only hope that the look on my face doesn't betray my thought.

For cash-flow purposes, knowing the length of the job is *necessary*. It becomes the schedule. If you can't answer that question, you are not prepared in my opinion to start, or in some cases, complete a project. And without a schedule, you might as well just guess about the budget you think you'll need to complete the project.

I inform the interior designers with whom I work that they must have a discussion with their clients regarding budgets and schedules before the job begins.

Once a schedule has been determined for the job, then you can move onto a fee structure. Anyone that knows me knows that I don't care about the method by which you invoice if you are billing for the work you are doing. If you have a yearlong project, the first thing you need to know is how much of your total fee you will be billing each month. If you cannot give at least rough numbers, then you are not prepared to start the job because I guarantee that your client will be asking you the same question. And you should be prepared for your client to ask these questions, especially for larger projects. It is a sign they are budgeting their cash flow. When you can answer these questions, it shows your client that you respect their money. Also, they will be less surprised when you submit your invoice. As the CFO, I am sometimes brought into the project to help answer that exact question.

Once you determine your total fee for a project and how much you expect to bill each month, you'll want to turn your attention to your purchasing budget. You should have reviewed with your client the items and materials that they intend to have installed in each room. Again, these numbers can be rough estimates, but it is important for your cash-flow projection to have an idea of the cash needed each month from the client in order for you to pay for the items that will be installed.

2020

Project A	January	February
Time Billing	10,000.00	10,000.00
Purchasing	250,000.00	200,000.00

Now that you have a schedule and budget, you can project roughly the amount of time and money needed per month to get the work completed. The easiest way to detail that information is to enter the amount that you expect to bill to your client each month into a simple spreadsheet, as shown above. Next, take your purchasing budget and enter by month how much you expect to receive from your client. (Note: When you are asking for money for furniture, for example, you need to keep in mind the lead times on orders for each item.) As you are entering this data, watch how your spreadsheet starts to tell you a story. Maybe I have been doing this work too long, but to me, numbers always tell a story.

For every job you are working on, a few simple functions in the spreadsheet will total all the time billing and all the purchasing by month. By the way, the computation might be the first time you have seen all your jobs in numbers.

I have some clients that do this monthly and when the totals by month start to get above a certain threshold, they start feeling overwhelmed. Usually this reaction means that they do not feel they have enough staff to handle all this work. You want to trust your gut when you feel like this.

Typically, the next question that comes my way after my clients feel this sense of being overwhelmed is "Can my firm sustain a new employee?" My response is "Let's review your next six months of incoming cash to find the answer."

Time Billing-Total	$	10,500.00
Purchasing-Total	$	25,000.00
TOTAL Cash Inflow	$	35,500.00
Estimate COGS	$	16,750.00
Overhead(Monthly Nut)	$	11,199.82
Owner Draws	$	4,516.97
Projected Net Profit	$	3,033.21

Those other additional line items are extremely important, however. In the accounting world, the largest expense usually of any project is what we call "Costs of Goods Sold" or COGS for short. You can just call them the amounts you need to pay your vendors. We must estimate this number in our cash flow example since most of vendor payments are made after your client pays you, the designer. These costs do not always manage to land in the same month your money is being received. To get an estimate you can use the mark up (known as your "margin") on your project that you normally make. For example, your margin on the cost that you will bill to your client—your selling price—might be 25 percent. In that case, 75 percent of the selling price would be dedicated to vendor costs, freight, etc.

Let's review the projected net profit, which is your cash flow, at the bottom of the above spreadsheet. In your own spreadsheet, is this number a large negative number or a large positive number? In accounting, positive numbers don't always mean great things.

Having a large positive cash inflow could mean that you have more work than you have staff to handle it. Watch that number as a sign that you might need to hire staff—or get more projects.

If you have more work than your staff can take on, you will lose out on billable time because deliverables according to the schedule are not being met, which will then in turn have a negative effect on your cash flow. The whole reason we go through this exercise is to determine cash flow. If you can't bill time, then the cash is not going to flow.

If you have a large negative number in your cash flow, you probably can guess what that means. You basically need more work to bill in order to fund your business (or cut staff). If you have listened to my podcast with LuAnn Nigara (episode #361), you will know that I believe that the way to fund your company consistently is through billing your time. You can project the time on jobs that you take on, but you can't project if those jobs will produce a profit by the purchasing budgets. Not all purchasing monies will result in guaranteed profitability. Therefore, we never want to rely on purchasing revenue from clients to fund our businesses.

Estimates

When I started in construction in my twenties, I was not in an accounting or finance division. I worked in a job trailer for a large project at an Oregon job site with a bunch of engineers. I worked on submittals and requests for information. Those functions are as boring as they sound, especially for someone who did not major in or want a career in engineering. The finance trailer on this job site interested me because that work dealt with all the estimates and accounting. Every time I would visit that trailer, I would ask more and more questions about how much this project cost. The staff was so annoyed with my constant questions that they finally gave me a project to work on that had something to do with finance and accounting. Suddenly, I was tasked with making money on the recycling. The construction projects were producing large quantities of wasted rebar, concrete, cardboard, plastic, etc., and the company did not want to throw it in the landfill. Being in Oregon, the commitment to recycle was serious business. The desire to make money at recycling these materials also was serious business. Challenge accepted. Also, it gave me something else to do besides submittals and requests for information.

Tasked with this new job, I was hungry to get my hands on information about recycling. My undergrad degree was in political science. What did I know about making money in recycling metal or cardboard? Little, if anything. Back then, the internet was new, and you could not Google "recycling for money." The job involved a lot of combing through the yellow pages. Every time that I obtained data, I entered it into a spreadsheet. I completed three scenarios of how much my company could receive in income based on how much we recycled. In some cases, the more we recycled, the less money could be expected and vice versa. Everything just depended on what the product was that was available to recycle at the time. Honestly, I was surprised at how much wasted rebar was worth. Until that point, I had never been so excited to look in dumpsters in all my life.

After reviewing my complied data, we implemented my program and started making some money from recycling. As the recycling progressed and we were making money, we were able to compare how much we were making based on the estimate that we had created for the program from my spreadsheet. It would not have been possible to know the performance accuracy of the recycling program without the original estimate for comparison.

Construction and architectural businesses would not be able to be run profitably without the use of estimates. Interior design companies are no different. I was very surprised when I got into interior design accounting that only 25 percent of my designers were completing estimates before starting a job. I needed to prove to my designers that estimates would be worth their time.

As I explained to each of my design clients, if you don't know your numbers, your client isn't going to know either. You need to be able to explain to your client how much their project is going to cost to complete. It is amazing how fast a client will pay a bill when they feel they understand where their money is going! Completing an estimate will allow you to explain project costs with more confidence and detail so that the client can see what they are paying for. I have heard too many stories about my designers guessing what they think a project is going to cost. Most suffer the consequences of an inaccurate guess.

Whenever you meet with a new client, you want to start by completing a walkthrough of the project or a meeting to review what needs to be completed during the project. Take your measurements, get a copy of the drawings, etc. Whatever you need to do to get a description of the scope of the project. Ask your questions, and let your client know you need to review the data and come up with an estimate. If that discussion is not acceptable to your client, then I would not work with them. Their project is an investment, not a trip to Ikea.

Then start a new spreadsheet. Make a list of each room of furniture, materials, or decorations that will go in each room. See the following example.

Furniture Estimate	Purchasing			
	Low		High	
Lower Level	$	78,920.00	$	97,500.00
Sofa	$	3,500.00	$	5,000.00
Lighting	$	48,920.00	$	55,000.00
Cabinetry	$	20,500.00	$	30,000.00
Rugs	$	6,000.00	$	7,500.00

Always list the high and low selling price for each item that will be installed in each room. Remember that those numbers are not set in stone and may change, but that is why we call it an estimate. Don't forget to add in freight, fees, and sales tax to the cost.

Next, you need to go through each room and decide how much design time to allot to complete that room. Best practice is to split the purchasing and installation time from the design time. If you have several staff that will be working on this project, you will want to estimate how much time each staff member will take to complete their respective assignment, because each member of your team is likely at a different billable rate. Remember, these are estimates. You are not committing to these amounts or putting them in your contract with your client. If they do change dramatically as the project progresses, then most likely your client has asked for additional work or a change in scope. Once you have reached a comfortable estimate for the entire project, establish and add your profit margin, and you're ready to think about setting costs in your contract should the client accept your estimate.

I am sure that several of you who are reading this text are saying, "I don't bill hourly, so this information would not apply to me." Not correct. This exercise is even more important in that case because regardless of whether you bill a lump sum or fixed fee, you still will need to conduct this exercise to come up with the values for the total amount.

Occasionally, you'll decide that you won't continue with the project after creating the estimate, but the exercise is still great practice so you know how to determine how much projects will cost. If you do continue with the project, as the project moves along, you can compare your estimate with actual project costs and monitor your progress. Remember to go back to your client if the scope has increased or changed because the original estimate did not include those costs, and you do not work for free. The written estimate in this case can be proof to your client that the cost of their recent change of mind (scope) was not included in the original estimate.

I have been in interior design, construction, and architectural accounting for 20 years. A lot of what I have learned was in the field and not in a classroom. I have learned from mistakes; I have learned from my mentors. I have even had clients provide feedback, from which I have also learned. If I ever come across something that I do not know, I will read, research, and ask questions until I have fully understood what I did not know before.

It is important to not be paralyzed by your fears. Make sure you are honest with yourself and about the things that you do not know. Realize that you need to ask for help sometimes. You are not only in the business of interior design. You are in the business of being an entrepreneur, and you *specialize* in interior design.

You had a reason, or more than one, when you decided to go this route and not to work for someone else. Outsource those jobs that fall outside your specialty, knowing that if you decide to do them yourself, it might cost you more in the end.

Epilogue

I played soccer pretty much my whole life until I broke my leg playing it at the age of 31. I still coach the sport to this day because I love it so much. My point of telling all of you this is that after I broke my leg and I was not able to play anymore, I still figured out a way to be involved in soccer. I love it that much.

I have always felt that if I don't love what I am doing in life to the point of finding any way to continue doing it, then I probably should reconsider. Most of my clients feel that same way about interior design. They love what they do so much that they complete every task I give them with the same dedication and thoroughness that they give to running their businesses. You can listen to all the advice in the world, you can even believe some of it, but just remember that you are the only person in your life who truly knows why you are doing all this hard work. Sure, you are going to make mistakes, but there is a reason why you are still in business. You love it! Sometimes—often—that is all we need.

Here was the money line, in case you missed it: "As I explain to each of my design clients, if you don't know your numbers, your client isn't going to know them either."

There is so much in Kim's chapter to sit with, digest, and then

compare to how you are managing your own money, but that one line is really important. If you don't know your numbers, your client isn't going to know them either. How can any project really be on track without this information?

I know you have had a client who was either shocked at an invoice, tried to negotiate an invoice, or simply ended a project, citing, "Expenses got out of control."

I'm right, aren't I?

If you aren't talking about budgets with your clients before you start the project, there is only one reason. One.

And don't tell me it's because your clients won't talk about it.

The reason is **you** aren't comfortable talking about the budget.

I have three words of advice:

Get over yourself.

Okay, so that was my **Inside Voice.**

Let me try my **Outside Voice.**

"Please, my esteemed business colleague, this is not about you or your discomfort. Consider this a sacred responsibility to your clients. In order to honor them and to design for them a project they both love and can afford, as well as to provide them with an amazing experience, it is valuable for all parties involved to establish a reasonable budget at the outset of the project."

Better?

When you really—I mean **really**—think about it, what is the big deal? Do you actually believe any client prefers to get involved in a design project, of any size, and not know how much money they can expect to spend? I am seriously asking you to think about this. You, too, are a consumer. Consider any purchase you have made in your lifetime. Have you ever once preferred to not have an idea of the cost before you got involved? Do you not look at the bottom of the shoe for the price before you sweetly say, "Size 7, please?"

Have you ever thought to yourself, "Oh, what a great realtor! He spent weeks showing me $5 million houses. After that, he talked to me in detail, and we figured out my budget was $1 million!"

Or, "What an uncouth waiter! The nerve. Describing the delightful Chilean Sea Bass special and then, after I ordered it, he told me it was $38.95!"

It is a simple request. It is an actual need. Tell me the budget before I get involved—before I get too far in.

Respect your clients, their time, and money. Respect yourself, your time, and money.

Learn to talk openly about money, budgets, timelines, invoicing. It is a business transaction, after all. It is expected. And, more importantly, it is expected that you will lead this conversation.

I know the finance part of business can be tricky, but that is no excuse. You have to wrap your brain around it. My hope is, with Kim's help, you'll have a better understanding of these important concepts regarding your money. However, if it is still a bit fuzzy, that's okay. You might need to reread the chapter a few times, or you might need to get one-on-one help. It is 100 percent okay to not understand; it is 100 percent **NOT** okay to leave it at that. Call your CPA, call your bookkeeper, call Kim, heck, call Ghostbusters. Just call someone!

Ask them to answer every question you have, explain every detail of your finance reports, until you are a master. You can learn how to project your pipeline, analyze your cash flow, talk budgets, and set up client invoicing schedules. You can.

If you are hesitant, it is probably because you're overwhelmed and maybe you do have that icky feeling in your stomach. Please persevere. In my more than 600 interviews, the guests who have expressed the most pride, the most satisfaction, the most hopeful outlooks for their profitability and their long-term success are, to a one, the designers who have gone from fuzzy to confident in their finances. I'm not usually one for "always" and "nevers," but in this case, it is true. For real-life examples and inspiration, listen to the episodes featuring Lisa Gilmore, Shirry Dolgin, Cat French, and Kimberley Kay. Every one of these women told us how it was a complete game changer when she finally had clarity regarding the finances.

Lisa Gilmore enthusiastically told us about her "Finance Fridays" and how each week she looks forward to the meeting with her bookkeeper. It excites and energizes her to review her financial reports. Now, she makes decisions for her business based on real data, real numbers—not guesses.

There are others like these ladies. Ask your designer friends. When you hear the relief, the joy, the happiness in someone who has gone from unsure to confident, you will be a believer.

The path to great client collaborations, to profitability, and to achieving your goals is in the numbers.

I hope you are on this path. You deserve it.

-LN

About the Author

Kimberly, the owner of KMM Consulting, has found that accounting and finances seem to scare most interior designers. She helps them by going into their businesses and taking on the role of CFO. From there she teaches them how to really understand what they need to do in order to become successful as entrepreneurs as well as interior designers. Kim's specialty is helping designers with what she calls Project Revenue Accounting, which is how to manage the revenue of a project that is already in process.

KMM Consulting takes on clients from around the United States. Kimberly has 20 years of experience working in accounting for companies such as Swinerton Builders, WRNS Studio, and Martin Group. She has her Masters in Accounting from Golden Gate University located in San Francisco. KMM Consulting's clientele includes a diverse group of service based companies, with the main focus on small interior design, construction, and architectural firms. The goal of her firm is to make the businesses she works for as profitable as they can be by educating them on accounting, cash flow management, tax deductions, project reporting, and business management.

Kimberly Merlitti has been a featured guest on A *Well-Designed Business*® podcast episodes 361 and 442.

Section Three

Marketing & PR

CHAPTER 5

Darla Powell

Often, I hear: "Social media doesn't work for me. Why should I bother?"

Typically, my response is, "So, tell me, is it that your strategic plan, with quality content, consistent posts, immediate thoughtful responses to all comments, delivered with your unique point of view and cohesive branding, across platforms doesn't work, or is it that your random posts while watching Netflix don't work?"

Exactly.

Let's get real, shall we?

If you order furniture and accessories without doing a floor plan, when it doesn't fit, is it the furniture's fault?

If you dump boxes of tiles, plumbing fixtures, and lighting at a job site, when it isn't installed the way you wanted, is it the contractor's fault?

No ma'am, no sir.

Would you design without a plan? I'm betting that's a hard "no."

So, when we take a haphazard approach to our social media and it doesn't work, why do we think social media doesn't work?

Well, because it is not easy to develop a social media strategy. Understand it takes knowledge, effort, and time. Just like interior design, it requires expertise to be done well. And, like with our beloved clients, as their good taste does not translate into professional design skills, neither does our throwing some pretty pictures on Instagram translate to an effective social media plan.

Fortunately, Darla is here to teach us exactly why social media works and how to outline a practical plan. Listen as she explains her journey into owning both an interior design firm as well as a social media company. Her story and her success are not debatable; they are proven facts. Darla's accomplishments, in three short years, are nothing short of remarkable. Keep top of mind, though, she has not achieved this success by accident or by luck. Darla developed a plan, used sound principles, showed up with consistency and intention, dedicated hours and hours of work, and then, **voilà**, social media worked for her!

Another thing before we get to Darla's chapter, if somehow this is your first time meeting her, you are in for a treat. Darla mentions how she and her wife, Natalie, were the emcees for "LuAnn Live, It's About the Conversation." She earned this invitation for many reasons, not the least of which is her hard-earned expertise and her leadership but also because I love her tell-it-like-it-is personality and her laugh-out-loud humor. She and Natalie are, as Darla would say, **awesome sauce** people! I think as soon as you read her chapter, you will know what I mean.

-LN

Think You Don't Need Social Media?

Darla Powell

If I told you the only reason you're reading this chapter was because of social media marketing, would you believe me? Well, believe it!

Social media was literally the engine behind my lightning-fast midlife transformation. When I think about it, the rapidity of the change still kind of makes my head spin like a wingnut (see what I did there?). Three years ago, on March 17, 2017, I went from being a full-time police officer with 18-plus years tenure with the Miami Dade Police Department—*Detective-Sergeant Darla Powell at your service!*—to being the proud owner of Darla Powell Interiors (DPI).

Yes, you read that correctly: Cop-turned-interior-designer. At age 47, to boot. I had a badge and a gun and a taser. I ran after bad guys on the midnight shifts, arrested murderers, comforted victims, and wrote my share of tickets. Okay, maybe less than my share...but the point is, I did a lot of cop sh*t for 18 years, and today, just a little over three years later, you're reading this chapter, my chapter, in the third book by LuAnn Nigara, host of the most influential and popular interior-design podcast. Today, I own both an interior design firm and a social media marketing agency, and I cohost my own social media marketing and business podcast, *The Wingnut Social Podcast*.

So how did I get from there to here? Charm and talent: 1 percent. Social media marketing: 99 percent.

Which brings me to the whole point of this chapter. I've talked with lots of interior designers who think they don't need social media. They just don't see the necessity of it all. Sound familiar?

I hear things like: It's just not effective.... High-end clients aren't on social.... I don't need it because all of my business comes from referrals.... It's just not a good investment of my time.... There's so much noise and competition.... It's just kid stuff....

I absolutely and wholeheartedly disagree! If you think that you don't need a strong presence on social media, allow me to gently and lovingly persuade you as to why you do and show you all of the benefits that social media can bring to you. Then, after I have successfully wooed you, I'll dig into exactly how to create a strategy for your social media presence to help you achieve your business goals. Are you game? Excellent! Let's do this.

What Social Media Can Do for Your Business

Since social media algorithms and platforms are ever-changing (job security for my marketing team at Wingnut Social), I'm not going to delve into technical nuts-and-bolts in this section because those elements will likely be out of date before this book gets printed. What I am going to dig into is all of the ways that this magical medium can get your name out there, build credibility, get you recognized as an expert in your industry, and...wait for it...get clients! You heard me. Real-life, living, breathing, paying design clients. Social media can do all that and more.

Social media can get your name out there.

When I traded in bullets for fabric swatches, I knew that I needed to make it known in a big way that I was in the design biz. Having been on Facebook personally for a while, I created a business page there—Darla Powell Interiors—and began relentlessly dive-bombing my friends and family and *their* friends and family with my intent to make their environments amazing. Word began to spread and soon friends of friends were hiring me to design and decorate their residences.

Like I did, you can get great results by focusing on 20-30 strong hashtags on Instagram and other platforms, as those key words are how new people find you. I spent hours commenting on other people's posts as a way to expose more people to my brand. And you know what? It worked! I saw fast growth on my accounts and started gaining traction.

Social media can help you build credibility, even with a limited portfolio.

As a "baby" designer ($1 to LuAnn) with a very limited portfolio, I needed some gravitas—some street cred. When potential clients visited my website and then inevitably moseyed over to my social channels, I wanted to impress the heck out of them with my social following, my engagement, and the aesthetic of my feeds.

My Instagram account quickly grew to 7,000 followers in a few short months due to my rabid (crazy?) diligence in posting and commenting. Potential clients would find me on social media, see my numbers there, and immediately assume that I was the real deal. That reach alone was enough to get them to pick up the phone and give me a call to get the conversation going.

But if you are a social media beginner, how do you begin?

When you have a limited portfolio, you have to be creative in finding content to post, which means you'll have to share posts of a lot of relevant material *other than* your finished original designs.

Depending on your brand, such posts might be quotes, pics of in-process projects, flatlays, travel photography, etc. The strategy part of this chapter (keep reading) will help you figure out exactly what to post and how often to do it, even if you don't have a ton of original design images.

Social media can bring in **new** clients and keep your pipeline full.

So, you think that no one gets new clients from social media? Alisa C. Popelka of Alisa Cristine Interiors in Dallas, who was a social media strategy client of Wingnut Social, would beg to differ. Alisa caught my eye originally on social just being all over the place! She is extremely diligent and consistent on her social channels—especially Instagram—and her efforts have paid off incredibly well. When I interviewed her on my podcast (episode 74), she divulged that she gets 50 percent of her design clients from social media—50 *percent*! Take that to the bank! Could you be leaving potential new clients on the table?

Almost all potential clients will check out your social media before contacting you, even if they were referred, and many are checking out multiple designers on social, which is why a strong, strategic social media presence that represents your brand well is so important. Potential clients will contact designers who have an active, engaged community, who show their personality as well as what working with them is like. That's how social works: the more you put out there, the more you get back.

Social media lets you show people exactly who you are.

One of the beautiful things about social media is that it's... well...social! There is no better way to show potential clients and collaborators *exactly who you are* on a daily or even weekly basis. Many, many people are tuning to their social media "drug of choice" daily if not hourly. Let's be honest, when was the last time you went to your favorite interior designer's *website* to see what he or she was up to? Exactly. Social is where we go to get to know, love, and trust each other—and that's the magic seed from which everything else grows.

I can't tell you how many clients have told me, "I feel like I already know you from Instagram! I love your videos and stories!" Those reactions are gold—literally! You are already "in" before you are even in. All you have to do next is have an amazing consultation and be yourself. They already love you and are most likely going to hire you if they can afford you. Connecting with potential clients is waaayyy easier to pull off with ongoing, daily/ weekly social media than that website you keep forgetting to update.

Of course, you don't get that attention by randomly posting about things that you like to do. You need a strategy (again, keep reading). Think about what you want people to know about your brand and what it's like to work with you. Then, figure out what kind of stories and bits of information that you can add into your posts to convey those attributes.

Video, for example, is especially great for helping people to get to know you, so don't be shy. "But Darla," I can hear you saying, "I hate being in videos and pics." I feel you, friend. It took me quite a while to get over myself and get comfortable appearing in images and especially on video. I still get a bit self-conscious and nervous, but now I (kinda) enjoy it. It has paid off in spades.

The more you practice and the more you do it, the easier it gets. I promise. When you watch one of your videos, look for spots where you appeared less than confident. Did you raise your pitch higher than your usual speaking voice (which is very common for us to do on camera)? Were you fidgeting? Using lots of speech fillers, like "uh" or "umm?" Pick out one thing to work on at a time. When you've fixed that issue, work on another one. If you focus on improving just one thing at a time, you'll improve so fast!

Social media can help you attract **ideal** clients.

My decidedly unique personality resonated with my social following and helped me to attract not just clients—but *ideal* clients with whom I genuinely enjoy working. We all know how important compatibility is! Can you imagine if that last nightmare client that you had to ditch (hey, it happens) had understood your aesthetic, how you work, and your personality up front? Maybe your mismatched and doomed-for-disaster vibes would have been obvious from the get-go, saving you untold grief.

More importantly, with a strong strategy, you'll attract your ideal tribe and repel the less-than-ideal who will skitter off to other pastures that better suit them. It's a beautiful, magical symmetry. But I've got to be honest: When I first started on this whole social media sojourn, and industry experts tried to tell me the same thing I'm telling you, I was highly skeptical (okay, I thought they were full of crap). But I'll be damned if it doesn't work—and work brilliantly.

All you need to do is to put yourself out there on social. Tell people who you are, what you do, what you like, and how you work, and you'll be amazed by whom you attract.

Social media can help you land high-end clients.

If I had a nickel for every time I've heard "high-end clients aren't on social"—well...I'd be retired and living in a Miami penthouse with a personal butler, trainer, and chef. The times are a-changin': People and luxury clients are all over social media. I promise you.

Interior design business coach and BOLD Summit's Grand High Pooh-bah, Julia Molloy, wholeheartedly agrees, advising even her own high-end-designer clients to be on social media. Julia had this advice to impart on the podcast: "Social media does play a part for luxury designers because it is part of their *street cred*. So, if you're wanting to be in editorials or be featured and out there in the media and part of that—certainly at least the building blocks to building that kind of global audience, whether it be video or editorial—is having that really strong online presence and that does include your social media."

Social media can help seal the deal even if all your business comes from referrals.

Anybody who is serious about hiring a professional like you will research said professional on digital media. Potential clients want to see more about *you* and your business. How is it to work with you? How do you comport yourself? How well do you interact with other clients and followers? How do you deal with negative feedback?

Answer this question: When was the last time you paid thousands of dollars to hire someone without scoping them out via everything you could get your hands on? Exactly.

Social media can help editors and producers find you.

Last year, I interviewed Abbi McCollum, VP for HGTV, on the podcast, and she was very clear that she and other HGTV executives regularly scour social to discover designers who are unique and different. Orlando Soria is a brilliant example of that type of discovery. (If you aren't already following him on Instagram, run! Don't walk.) His personality sets him apart, and that aspect is something that only the medium of social media could have showcased as effectively as it has. Be sure to watch him on HGTV. Just sayin'!

While I haven't yet landed a gig on HGTV (what the hell, Abbi?), my social media prowess has garnered the attention of multiple editors. Through social media, I met Natalie Reddell, who kindly listed the *Wingnut Social* podcast in ADPro (that's *Architectural Digest*, folks) as her favorite design-biz podcast. PureWow named me—DPI—one of the top Miami designers to follow on Instagram purely from finding me after I posted a new project shot. A similar promotion happened with Brightech, which listed DPI as one of the top design firms in Miami as well as one of the top design bloggers in 2019 after discovering and connecting with me on Instagram and Facebook. Being social pays off with free press and accolades, which in turn, adds to your credibility and impresses potential clients.

Where to start? Do your research on industry editors and publications and tag them in posts of your original designs that you'd like them to consider. Couple that tactic with traditional pitching and media relations. Even if those efforts don't turn into a feature in their publications, tagging editors and publications often leads to them sharing your content on their feeds, which results in a major boost in followers.

Social media can lead to speaking engagements (if that's your jam).

As my social media presence began to grow, I started to get noticed by design industry powerhouses. Through social networking, I met Mark McDonough (*Tastefully Inspired* blog) who introduced me to LuAnn Nigara, which resulted in my being on not one but two episodes of LuAnn's podcast. Then Natalie Grafe and I were invited to emcee the very first *LuAnn Live* event. And of course, now you're reading my chapter in this book.

In addition to getting LuAnn-related opportunities, I've been fortunate enough to be a guest on numerous industry podcasts and invited to speak at High Point Market (more than once!) with the likes of Corey Damen Jenkins, Nicole Heymer, Sandra Funk, Shayla Copas, Sasha Bikoff, and others.

Your first invitation to any media event creates a bit of a snowball effect and establishes one more way to attract and impress potential clients. If speaking engagements are among your goals, position yourself on social as the go-to expert in your chosen niche. Be persistent and tenacious. Tag the people or events that you're interested in and reach out. Social is networking on a grand scale.

Now What? Craft a Social Media Strategy

Okay, now that you're stoked and ready to get your social going (right?), you're going to need a solid strategy. Strategies keep you on track, help you meet your goals, and take the anxiety out of daily choices. Without a strategy, you're doing what we at Wingnut Social call "randomly throwing content at the wall to see what sticks." While social media feels fun and spontaneous, you don't want your posts to be random from a business standpoint. Good social media strategies are decision-making documents (yep, information that lives on paper, not just in your head) that you come back to time and time again when you've got decisions to make. So, how the heck do you come up with a solid strategy? Follow this simple (well, pretty simple) five-step recipe.

Step 1: Define Your Goals

I've talked about lots of ways that social can help your business. But you need to focus. What are the most important ways for *your* business? Do you want to drive traffic to your website? If so, Instagram probably isn't the best platform for you. But do you want to become an influencer and have potential clients see how "purdy" your interior designs are? Boom: Instagram will be your jam.

Your goals must be real *business* goals, however, not just social media goals. For example, getting more reactions and followers isn't really a business goal. It's nice and all, but the real question is: What do more impressions and followers help you achieve? Why would you even want that attention? What's your endgame? If brand awareness is your goal, on the other hand, that's a real business goal that social media can help you knock out of the park. Brand awareness would then become a major player throughout your strategy document.

Or perhaps your goal is to get more media attention and to become the next design superstar? Great! Outline strategies and tactics to achieve that goal. For example, look at the Facebook pages of other designers who are getting lots of clicks to see which editors and publications have shown interest on those pages and develop a list of them to target and tag in all of your social posts. Write down that list in your strategy document so you don't have to try to remember whom you're supposed to tag (because if you're anything like me—and Natalie—you *will* forget. P.S. Will someone please tell Natalie to write sh*t down? Thank you!).

Step 2: Do Your Research and Differentiate

In order to get the most out of social, you need to understand two things: (1) what you've done before (both what's worked and what hasn't), and (2) what your competitors are doing. You don't want to do the same thing they're doing because no one wants carbon copies. You want to set yourself apart, to put your unique spin on everything.

Some things to consider when researching your own performance:

- What are your top-performing posts for positive reactions? *Ohhh*, do more of that!
- What are your worst performing posts? *Let's not speak of those!*
- Notice any patterns? Is the image causing the reaction? The caption? The location that you tagged? *Take note!*
- Check what percent of non-followers see your posts. Aim for more than 50 percent. That level tells you how well your hashtags are working. If it's lower than 50 percent, definitely change your hashtags. To what, you ask? Take a look at the hashtags used by the top accounts in your

industry both locally and nationally (don't tell them I tipped you off). And keep experimenting with mixtures of popular hashtags, niche hashtags, and location hashtags.

- Which kinds of posts get the most engagement? Look for patterns. Are the posts that are getting the highest and lowest engagement the same as the ones getting the highest and lowest reactions? If the interactions are different, you need to understand why.

Some things to consider when examining your competitors' social accounts:

- Do they share personal information? Are they revealing their unique personality? Does personal appeal seem to be successful for them? (Hint: Yes, *it's successful for them unless they're, well, awful.*)
- Do they provide design tips? Do they hold back a little or tell all?
- What's the engagement rate on their posts (if you can still see the numbers of "likes," in that Instagram is sporadically experimenting with hiding "likes")?
- Do they have a consistent aesthetic? If yes, how can you differentiate yourself from that aesthetic (e.g., you focus on pics with bold color in the accents to differentiate yourself from someone with a white and bright aesthetic)? Of course, your aesthetic needs to be your true style (no carbon copies or clones, remember?), but sometimes you can make choices to create your aesthetic.
- How would you describe someone who would want to follow a competitor's feed? Is he or she slightly different (or very different) from whom you want to attract?
- Are your competitors' clients the same as your ideal clients? To what kind of aesthetic and color palette is your ideal client drawn? Are those elements the same as your preferred aesthetic and color palette?

Again, write down your findings in your strategy document. (*Don't pull a Natalie and try to "remember" it in your head. I even bought her a journal! Sigh....*)

Step 3: Nail Down Your Positioning

Now that you've looked at what works and what doesn't, you need to formulate the best way to position yourself on social media. No need to bring out the slide rules. Not that kind of formula. Also, this determination isn't just a list of what your business does. It's a statement of what sort of person—or persona—that you or your business should project on social media as well as what you will offer to your followers.

At Wingnut Social, we sometimes get at those answers by asking clients: "If you were on an HGTV show, who would you be? Would you be the confident boss giving orders? The one crying when things don't turn out right? The funny one keeping everyone happy while still working hard? The super-creative one? The one who ignores what the client says that they want? The guy eating the cockroach off the floor?" (Did you catch that one? I almost died! But I digress.)

Think of a Venn diagram—you know, those round, intersecting, pie-shaped diagrams. You want to find the overlap between *how you want to be seen* and *how you really are*. That intersection is who you should be on social media. Think *curated authenticity*. Write it up in a paragraph. Or two.

Next, think about why someone would want to follow that person. What will you offer to your followers? Pretty pictures are a good start, but they're not enough. What do your competitors offer their followers? How can you offer something a little different? Or more? Or better? This area is your value proposition.

For example, do they get a behind-the-scenes look at the life of a designer? Or info about local art?

Once you have those two parts nailed down, there are two more things to consider: Your voice and your aesthetic. Write out how you/your brand should "sound" and "look" on social to deliver on your positioning and value proposition. Include adjectives to describe your voice, and make a separate list of adjectives to describe your aesthetic.

Now that you have that groundwork, the rest is easy. All of your strategies and tactics need to deliver on those four parts. You don't have to wonder every day what you should do. Does this post deliver on my positioning and value proposition? If yes, post it. If no, don't. (*Or do. Just don't say I didn't warn you.*)

Step 4: Choose Your Content Pillars and Content Mix

Create a list of different types of bits and pieces that you could post to help deliver on your value proposition. Just brainstorm a list of blue sky options. That list will change a lot based on your specific positioning.

Here are a few examples:

- Vacation pics
- Posts about my family
- Design events that I attend
- Inspirational quotes
- Business quotes
- Design tips
- Flatlays and mood boards
- Pics of me
- Exteriors of homes
- My finished designs

- Art
- In-progress design projects
- Pics of me with whiskey
- More pics of me with whiskey
- Pics of me and Natalie with...whiskey

Ask yourself why each category is necessary to help achieve your goals. Ask yourself if each category helps to fulfill your positioning and value proposition, and to reach your target audience. If not, cut it. For example, if you want to be known by local architects, posting exteriors of homes may help you achieve that goal. Now, ask yourself if your list is sufficient to cover everything that you should deliver on. Is there anything that you need to add?

Ta-da! You now have the types or categories of content you'll provide—otherwise known as your content pillars. List them out for each social media platform. And list them for each aspect of Instagram (feed, stories, IGTV). Not all pillars will work for every platform.

The next part is where you define your content mix, which is the frequency of each content pillar. For example, on your Facebook feed, you may have 5 percent in-progress design images, because they don't perform that well on most feeds, but 50 percent on your Facebook stories because you want to show what your process is like.

For an Instagram feed, our team at Wingnut Social recommends four to seven posts per week for designers, so base your percentages on the assumption of that frequency. Choose the frequency that works for you. You can always increase your frequency; you should never decrease it.

Now, planning your content will be *soooo* easy. For example, you know that you need to publish one quote per week. In your social media management software or on a spreadsheet, pick a day each week for a quote, and put the actual quote into your planner. You need a vacation pic each week? Again, choose a day for a vacation pic and follow through with it, figuring out which one you want to use each week. You don't need to write captions at this stage, just figure out what you'll do for each post. Continue until your whole month is planned.

Step 5: Think About Hashtags and Tags and Captions

The devil's in the details, right? Other bits of info you should plan out include particulars such as which hashtags and tags to use. Create a thorough list that resonates with and helps achieve your goals. If your goal is to connect with manufacturers, include manufacturer-related hashtags. Want to get speaking engagements? Get specific editors to notice you? Develop a hashtag and tag strategy to support those goals and write them down.

Once that nitty-gritty is out of the way, you can move on to captions. I've found that shorter captions work well, but some really successful designers are known to write mini-novels for their captions! Orlando Soria is one who uses the *looooooong* caption technique. If you go that route, just make sure to really grab the reader's attention within those first few words. On Instagram, only the first (roughly) 125 characters show up before someone has to tap "read more." Say something that will really smack them in the face and get them to stop, read, like, and follow.

Finally, Think About Outsourcing Your Social Media to Experts

I get it. Doing social media correctly—going through those five steps—is a big time investment (and it's easy to fall down deep rabbit holes). In the beginning, I had all the time in the world to do my own social because my client load was low. But when you do get too busy, you really should consider lowering your control-freak flag and delegating your social marketing "outside of your scope of genius," as Gay Hendricks, author of *The Big Leap* suggests. (I highly recommend his book, by the way. It made a huge difference in my biz mindset.) I know that delegating can be incredibly challenging for creatives like us, but when you think about spending one more minute at your current hourly rate on your iPhone doing social? Yeah, how about...no.

Awesome Sauce!

I hope this chapter that LuAnn has so graciously invited me to write has set off a light bulb or two or three for you, especially if your feet were firmly planted in the referral-only land before you began reading.

❖ ❖ ❖

I absolutely, truly, one million percent believe that not only is a strong and strategic social presence necessary to any business, but it's vital. It has opened so many doors and opportunities for me and for Natalie, and it can do the same for you. See you @ wingnutsocial!

With gratitude, Darla

Her first line tells it all. Darla is a coauthor in this book specifically because of social media. Let's trace the steps. First, Darla found my podcast A Well-Designed Business® through social media. This was, in small part, the germ of the many things to come for Darla and her entrepreneurial journey.

You see, listening to the show, month after month, ignited in Darla what was already in her. She had the talent, the desire, and the drive necessary to be an interior designer. At the end of 2016, Darla emailed me and told me, fortified by the podcast, she made a huge decision. She was changing careers after 18 years and launching Darla Powell Interiors.

This impressed me.

And it made an impression on me.

Meanwhile, I had already met Mark McDonough, also through social media, and we became fast friends. In fact, Mark was a coauthor in volume one of this **Power Talk Friday** book series. Simultaneously, also through social media, Mark and Darla met each other.

Fast forward, Mark is telling me about this amazing Darla Powell who is killing it on social. I think to myself, wait, is this the same designer who had emailed me only a few months before telling me she was **about** to launch her firm?

Full circle, the three of us connected, all through social media!

Listen to both of Darla's episodes on the podcast, #203 and #330. The entire story and timeline are pretty amazing and a pretty compelling endorsement for the powerful possibilities of social media.

One last caveat.

You have to have the business chops to back up the opportunities you create. Since social media marketing can grow quickly, first you have to be ready. Priority one is always to prepare your business, then grow your pipeline. You have heard me say before, you have to be prepared to be lucky.

This applies whether we are working to grow our gross revenue start-up to $100,000, or from $3 million to $5 million. Each level of growth requires certain processes and systems to be in place. Meaning, if you have a social media strategy that brings in many new clients or new clients above your current level of expertise, your business processes and systems must be able to support the increased demand while maintaining an excellent experience. Otherwise, you risk doing far more harm than good to your business and specifically to your profits.

Imagine you invite 20 people to an exclusive, formal sit-down dinner in your home. Everyone is excited, including you. You love to host dinner parties...you do it all the time. This is your first one for 20 people, though, and you think "I know what I'm doing." Your guests begin to arrive, they've put on their "Saturday night" outfit, they have their lovely hostess gift in hand, excitedly they ring your doorbell, brimming with anticipation at the incredible evening they are about to have. It's magical. Yet, when the door opens, you are frantically setting the table, your laundry baskets are in the corner, your kids are running around, and you're in your yoga pants. Nervously, you smile, you explain, you are working very hard, it took more time than you thought, just have a seat, it'll be fabulous, I promise.

This isn't a fabulous party. You are not ready. Your guests are disappointed, possibly mad. Your invitation was beautiful, the description of the evening was alluring, and it felt special, but in reality, it is none of these things.

This is what happens when you focus on driving new clients to you but do not have your business set up on the back end to properly handle them. When your social media promises something to potential clients, you need to deliver on that promise.

Set yourself up to succeed. Lock down your process. Next, either get to work on your social media plan with Darla's advice or work directly with Wingnut Social. Build your platforms, attract your ideal clients, get the world to bang down your door. Then, wow them when they do.

-LN

About the Author

Darla has a fun, genuine, and down-to-earth approach to the designing of beautiful spaces. Since she launched her career in 2016, she has grown her business almost exclusively by social media marketing and her clients have really fallen in love with her work!

In her past life, Darla spent almost 20 years as a Detective Sergeant in Miami, Florida, so one might say that she is an expert on the importance of having complete tranquility at home after a stressful day at work! Also, her background has carried over many hidden perks—including a strong sense of integrity, accountability, and a ready-for-anything-ness that is key for home renovation projects.

Darla's career transformation was fueled by her need to express her boundless creativity. She spent her childhood summers rummaging through her grandmother's antique store where she developed an extensive knowledge of antiques, of collectibles, and of pieces that look perfect together, so Darla's refined eye definitely sees those diamonds hiding in the rough! Above all, Darla really loves creating rooms that are gorgeous, elegant, and soothing.

Darla Powell has been a featured guest on *A Well-Designed Business*® podcast episodes 203, 330, and 601.

CHAPTER 6

Amanda Berlin

There's something about a Jersey girl. I think it's the Jersey energy. No matter what it is, when I met Amanda, we clicked. I remember being so impressed when she told us on the podcast if you are going to do a show house, have a specific PR plan. So simple, so direct, so obvious, yet, how many times in my own career at Window Works had we not done this?

We have participated as the window treatment vendor in many show houses over the years, including several times in the big daddy, Kips Bay, as well as The Hamptons Show house, The Mansion in May, and the Valerie Fund Show house. Yet not once had we thought to leverage the PR opportunities surrounding this investment. Blindly, we thought our participation in the show house was enough. As you know, it is thousands of dollars to participate in a show house. From Amanda, I learned to not maximize that investment with a thoughtful PR strategy is foolish and shortsighted. Talk about an "aha" moment!

Amanda also impressed me because she was the first PR rep I met who would do a one-off project, exactly like a campaign for a show house. Prior to this, I considered PR a yearly investment, built on a retainer business model. Offering PR services on a project basis is genius. It enables both the new and seasoned entrepreneur to leverage opportunities that would otherwise be missed. Don't misunderstand me: I do believe in the value of a long-term PR campaign and in working with a professional to guide you and to execute it for you. This is beneficial especially when you can both afford it and have the point of view and work experience to warrant it. However, so many opportunities exist along the path to this stage in your business that could be seized to propel your business forward.

Before you read Amanda's chapter, I'd like to ask you to do a small experiment with me. Answer this question right now: Who is a designer, with a practice similar to my own, that I learned of only through social media, speaking engagements, podcast appearances, print and digital placements, and/or brand collaborations?

Eliminate the "A-list designers" like Nate Berkus and Corey Damen Jenkins...they are super stars that we may know and do love, but I'm not talking about these men and other designers like them who are regularly found in HGTV, AD 100, Elle Décor, etc. I'm talking about your everyday, garden-variety peers.

Who comes to mind?

Several come to my mind, and at the end of this chapter I will share a few with you about them.

For now, as you read the chapter, reflect on the designers who came to your mind and relate Amanda's lessons to what you know about them. I am certain you will see in them the elements Amanda teaches us about being visible, about creating authority, about building your business through public relations.

-LN

Why You? How to Tell Your Story

Amanda Berlin

Are you connecting with people you *really* want to work with?

Do you feel confident and that you can fully express yourself when you put yourself out there?

Do you feel inspired when you hear *yourself* tell others about your own work and your professional journey?

I know that you are so passionate. And you are here for a reason. You have so much talent, wisdom, and so much experience to offer the world. Yet you, like most of us, can get trapped so easily in the loop of "no one cares what I have to say." Or believing, "I'm just out there with the same message as everyone else has, so why would they want to buy *from me*?" With such negative thinking, we can actually start to self-destruct and sabotage our success— sometimes before our work even gets off the ground.

Now before you stop listening, deciding I'm not talking about you, see how you answer the following questions.

Do you find yourself tripping over your words when you talk about what you do?

When you hear yourself describing yourself and your work, does it just not sound as good coming out of your mouth as it did in your head?

Do you often feel frustrated, even angry, about the lack of progress that you're seeing?

Are you uncertain about what you can do to turn things around?

If you answered yes to even just one of those questions, I want you to know you're in the right place.

You have bigger dreams, you've shown up because you're really tired of feeling invisible, and you want a business that supports you. Enough is enough!

Today is the day that those feelings begin to turn the tide in your favor.

Who Am I?

Hi! I'm Amanda Berlin. I'm a former corporate publicity strategist who now uses my powers for good (LOL). After 12 years in the world of corporate public relations agency work, I realized that the skill I had honed working on behalf of large corporations was completely transferable to small businesses and solo entrepreneurs. I had learned, over 10,000 hours of practice, how to create a story that balanced my clients' needs to "get the word out" with the media's need for good content.

Back then, we weren't paying for ad space. We were offering useful information in exchange for free airtime. My job was to balance what my client wanted to say "out there" with messages that their spokesperson could convince the media to deliver along with the regular news to their viewing audiences.

That approach is the *exact* same formula that each of us, as business owners, can employ on behalf of our own businesses: take a message, pair it with a spokesperson (*yourself*), and pitch it to the media.

But, there was a time when I didn't feel like I was ready for primetime. I was operating my business, but I "forgot" to use my magic on myself.

I was having one of those "aha" moments. "Not enough people know about ME!" I whined to a friend.

I lamented hearing from owners of businesses like mine—and whom I knew—during podcasts on which I should have been. I wanted to get my message out there too.

"So, pitch yourself," my friend said. Sometimes another's comment is all it takes—a nudge from a trusted advisor to get you to take action.

I sent the pitch.

Almost immediately, I received an email back. "Let's get you on the show," wrote John Lee Dumas, from *Entrepreneur on Fire*.

It worked! I just had to take the step.

In retrospect, I can't believe I was *that* surprised. Of course it worked! I'd been doing the same thing for other people for so long.

We *can* pitch ourselves to get the opportunities we want. Not only *can* we. We *must*!

Right now, the media climate is such that journalists, reporters, influencers, podcasters *want* to hear from YOU—not a third-party mouthpiece that you hired to do your pitching for you.

Just as I did in my previous career, today, I work with *my* clients to help them find their story, craft their messages—unique points that only *they* can make, stories that only *they* can tell. (Those details are what set you apart!!! We'll get to that.) And then I help them find the places to be seen and heard so that they connect with more of the right clients.

My clients have enhanced their profiles exponentially as a result of our working together. Publicity begets publicity. Visibility momentum is a "thing." You have to cultivate it. You have to put a strategy in place, and you have to stay the course. The complete package takes time!

My hope for you in reading this advice is that you feel inspired to champion your own worth, herald your own work, and sing your own praises. I want you to fall back in love with your work (and yourself, your journey, your story) so much that you can't wait to start talking about all of it in a new way, with new energy.

I will show you how.

Here's what I intend to offer you in this chapter:

- I will help you find your point of view—your stake-in-the-ground belief about what is possible through your work;
- We'll uncover the essential story structure that will inspire your clients and give you confidence when you talk about what you do;
- You'll learn how to create two distinct story ideas that you can pitch virtually anywhere so that you can burst out of your word-of-mouth bubble and be known by more people who want to work with you;
- You'll acquire the essential media-mindset tricks that will get you mentally ready for your close-up.

By the time you finish reading this chapter, you will feel comfortable getting out there with a new story about *you* and *your* work as well as new ways to wrap your head around getting seen, interviewed, and featured.

What Is Your Point of View?

What does it mean to have a point of view? Simply put, having a point of view means no longer having that anxiety dream in which you're screaming but no one hears.

We all know that feeling. Maybe you've even had that kind of dream. But certainly when you pour your passion into your work, you know the *frustration* of feeling like you're screaming into the abyss and no one is hearing you.

How often have you seen people whose work is similar to yours getting jobs that you *know* you could do, and being heralded for their work in publications that you *know* you should be a part of?

Having a point of view means you don't get ignored in a crowded field.

When you have a clear point of view, potential clients know when to turn to you and for what experience. They know what kind of work that you do best. They know your aesthetic, your style, and what it's like to work with you. They also can immediately tell that you are the right choice for them. And because they understand the kind of work—and perspective—you offer, they also can immediately refer the friends of a friend or business associates to you.

Having a point of view means you don't feel frustrated, muted, stifled, or unheard.

It's a basic human need to be seen, heard, and understood. We are relational creatures. Not only do we crave connection, we need it in order to feel complete. As much as we want to find our point of view in order to distinguish ourselves, we need to find it so that we feel fully expressed, having adequately articulated what we intend to do with our lives and careers.

Having a point of view is more than merely important.

You have something unique to contribute to this world, and if you don't find your voice, the *world* will be incomplete. People are out there who are waiting to hear from you. Projects out there awaiting your touch. If you don't step forward into the importance of your voice and vision and the possibilities that abound, there will be a "you shaped" void where you otherwise could have had an impact.

You will be incomplete. You will go on constantly feeling like there is more you could and should be doing, more you could be sharing and more beauty that you could be offering to the world.

Worse, you will not be seen for the absolutely essential and unique viewpoint as it relates to the service/product that you have to offer. If you don't find your point of view, your vision for your life and business will falter. You will miss opportunities that could change the trajectory of your business. You will continue to take shots in the dark and go out with broad messages that resonate with no one. Your business will not move forward.

Remember the old adage (or Katy Perry's lyric in "Roar") that if you stand for nothing, you'll fall for anything. It's true in business as well. If you don't take a stand and claim your point of view, no one will know what you do, who you can help, and how you might be able to transform their space (and their lives)! People won't know whom to refer your way either.

I dive deep with my clients into creating their stake-in-the-ground point of view and key messages. I want you to answer just a few questions for yourself to start to build your point of view. You can jot them down in the margins of this book or in your favorite work journal. This exercise will help you figure out what makes you uniquely different.

Time to Shake, Rattle, and Roll!

Let's write your "Big, **Bold,** I Believe" statement.

To start, complete these statements:

I teach people to _____.

This information changes their lives because _____.

If you were having a foot-stomping, fist-shaking moment while talking about what you do, what would you be saying about what you believe?

I believe _____.

Once you've polished those statements, you can put them into your mission statement and other appropriate places on your website. Remember also to weave them into conversations that you have with people about what you do!

What **Is** Your Story?

Sounds like an aggressive lead-in, right? Especially if you're from New Jersey, it could be a threat! Actually, it might feel like a threat anyway if you don't know how to tell your story in a way that supports your business.

Let's figure out how you can use your story to inspire those around you. Let's use your story to create a connection with people who are your perfect clients. We'll begin with a structure that will help you frame your story in a way that makes it easy for an audience of your prospects to digest.

What does framing your story mean exactly? It means that you create a narrative so meaningful to your audience that they couldn't possibly sit there, furrowed-browed, wishing you would just get to the point or fall victim to that glazed-over, deer-in-headlights look. It means you will have a plan that really connects with your audience. Having the right structure means you will know *exactly* where to go in your mind and what to say when someone asks the question, "What do you do?"

Connecting to potential clients and creating relationships form the backbone to every thriving business. They go hand-in-hand and beyond those people you already know. When I talk about relationships, I mean the ones you need to create outside your existing sphere of influence (while not neglecting those within your circle). Telling the *right* narrative about yourself and your work can invigorate a whole new population of clients, *and* it will make them feel engaged with and connected to you. Without it, you end up tripping over your words and veering off course.

You'll also miss strategic opportunities to distinguish yourself. Your story might be *the* one factor to a prospective client that separates you from other professionals in your category. Think of it as your own personal snowflake unlike any other personal and professional expertise out there. No one has done all the things that *you* have done the way that *you* have done them. Make your story your best advocate in business.

You also must utilize your story at every opportunity. Otherwise, you're sacrificing the information that inevitably sets you apart. You will continue to be another person selling the same service. You'll see opportunities go to other people. The chance to communicate your legacy will disappear. I know that you didn't start your business to fail, so polish and rehearse your delivery of your narrative until you can repeat it automatically whenever the occasion arises.

When I work with clients, creating their story is one of the first tasks that we undertake. It's paramount and essential to all the subsequent visibility work we do, like pitching the media, speaking to an audience, or sitting for an interview. Your story is meant to foster alliances. What I recommend that you do first is to get clear on your narrative as it relates to your work. Never share anything you haven't fully processed yet. You need to be able to deliver your story in a structure that's easy to digest. The easiest way to create a story structure is a simple before-and-after format. The three-act narrative is the way we've been consuming stories for eons.

Here's your work for this section.

Write your story in three acts, or as a simple before and after message, to include the following answers:

Where were you before you found the work you're doing today? Who were you? What did you believe? How did you live?

What was the catalyzing moment that changed everything for you? What epiphany did you have? What moment changed your life forever?

Where did you land after that? Where did that change take you? How do you work differently now? How did that adjustment lead you to where you are today?

Answer those questions for yourself and massage the answers

into a story that speaks to all that you are.

The Only Two Pitches You Need

Now, when I tell you that it's time for you to start writing your pitches, what do you think about? How do you feel? Overwhelmed? Unprepared? Completely lost? What if I narrowed your focus so that you only have to dream up two pitches? Would that clarification feel much more doable?

Well, it's true: You only need two basic pitches, and they are the "how-to" pitch and the "profile" pitch. You can (and must) customize them for the outlet you want to reach.

I'm going to give you examples of each, a basic outline for each, and the media venues where each story would be most well-received.

The "How-To" Pitch

I'll give you a quick primer:

Your **"how-to" pitch** is one in which you will teach the audience. In all likelihood, you have a lot of content, and certainly a lot of ideas, that could be used in your how-to pitch. It's a story idea based on your expertise that you can offer in an "of service" manner to a reading, listening, or viewing audience.

The basic "ask" is as follows:

You are asking the podcaster, reporter, influencer, producer, decision-maker: would your audience be interested an [interview/article/segment/feature] on *How to Make Great Color Choices for*

Dining Rooms That Will Translate for Every Season.

Make sure to issue the request in the form of a headline that they can envision actually using in the context of the their respective medium.   Next, put your idea in the format that is familiar to them so that they can see how easily you can produce it for them. For example, if your target is a [_____].

Targets for Your How-To Pitch

The "how-to" pitch works best in:

- Magazines articles that appear as short snippets in the "front of book;"
- Television segments where you can demonstrate or showcase a certain visual "how-to;"
- Newspaper articles in the lifestyle or home and garden section;
- Websites of well-known suppliers or manufacturers of materials that you use in your product/service.

The "Profile" Pitch

Your **profile pitch** is about you, your journey to create your business, your expertise, and is where your point of view is super-important. In your profile pitch, you need to make a case for yourself as a visionary—or at least a fresh perspective—in your line of work. Use your before-and-after story structure here, and lean into your particular point of view.

Targets for Your Profile Pitch

This pitch works best in:

- Podcast and radio interviews where the running time is longer enabling a deeper dive*
- Local magazines that feature resident business owners
- Local newspapers in the style or business section

----

*Note that these interviews can be a hybrid of your story/ journey and what you can teach to an audience (your "how-to" pitch).

Template for Your Pitch Structure

Dear [name],

My name is [name and link to website]. I am a [specialty here], who does [your service/product here] with/for [audience here].

I personally appreciate your work in providing [kind of information] to [specific audience]. Your recent interview with [name of guest] resonated with me because [personal connection].

I'm writing to you with an idea for an [article/interview] on: [headline here].

[Set up the story. Use the language you might imagine the interviewer using to introduce you.]

I can see us talking about the following: [include possible talking points bulleted].

I have written on this topic [link here] and [here]. I've been interviewed/appeared [here] and [here].

[Insert any relevant details about yourself here that make you perfect to address this topic].

I hope to hear from you to set up an interview.

Best,

[your name]

[your business name and contact information]

————————————

Note: Also include your business card in your letter.

Media Success Stories

Melina Palmer is an expert in behavioral economics who wanted to get a book traditionally published. She was told by an agent that she needed to build her platform to be considered by publishers. We set about getting her a column and "contributor-status" in *Inc.* magazine by carefully curating the many ideas she had into headline-worthy submissions that *Inc.* could see in its publication.

Jamie Lieberman, a coauthor of this very book, is an attorney and owner of an all-female, virtual law practice. Jamie had a big paradigm-shifting idea about work-life balance. We pitched her idea to *Working Mother* magazine and got Jamie's essay published. In turn, her being featured in a major magazine gave her idea tangible credibility and the confidence to run with it, which led to many other contributions spearheaded by a publicist whom she then hired to assist with the effort.

Karen Wilson is a clinical neuropsychologist who founded a platform meant to connect families with the resources needed to support their children with learning differences. Karen pitched her expertise to relevant podcast producers, was interviewed about her journey, how her platform works, and shared special how-to advice for families.

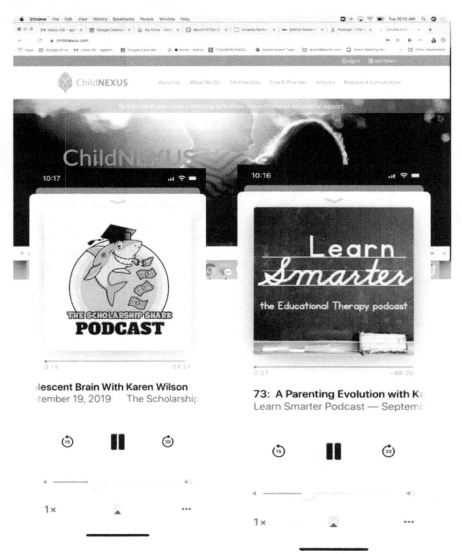

Judy Berlin is a local business owner, who happens to be my mom! Her fitness business was featured in a beautiful, local, glossy magazine in the town in which she lives. A resident business with a 30-year longevity is something that local magazines eat up. Their mandate is to write about local people. So, grab your free invitation to do the same. Pitch yourself!

Your Media Mindset

Inevitably, imposter syndrome will hunt you down, and you'll start to question whether you deserve to "be out there." That doubt is normal, but don't let it stop you. You do deserve to be out there.

When you begin your venture out into the public to become more visible and get more attention for yourself and your work, you need to remember the following three pillars of a successful media mindset, adapt them into your own media mantra to help you with your visibility confidence.

What Do I Need to Remember About Myself?

- I know my stuff;
- I have something that will be helpful to someone out there;
- I have studied and trained in order to possess this knowledge;
- Even some of the simplest details of my work could be mind-blowing for someone new to the conversation.

Never doubt that you have something valuable to contribute. You have an expertise that you have honed as well as a perspective that will open people's minds to something other than their own viewpoint. *Someone* out there is searching for you at this very moment! You studied and trained and put in your thousands of hours so that you could help that very person. If they can't find you (because you're not "putting yourself out there"), what a waste that would be! And finally, if you go back to the most basic elements of your expertise and learning over the years, those simplest of details would be enough to enlighten someone who's new to your work.

What Do I Need to Remember About the Decision-Maker?

- They have a job to do, and that job is to bring good content to their audience;
- They are actively searching for good leads, sources, and story ideas;
- They need us;
- We are a valuable asset to them and contribute to their success.

Many times, we reject ourselves before we allow someone else to even have a say in the decision. In this part of our mindset work, I want to remind you about who those decision-makers are. The ones to whom you are reaching out have their own job to do, and that job involves creating a lot of content. They can't do that alone! They need ideas and people like you to provide novelty. They are in a near-constant search for good leads, great story ideas, and dependable sources on whom they can rely. As a professional source of great information and ideas, you can create a relationship with a reporter, podcaster, television, or radio producer that will pay off over time. Remember: they need you!

What Do I Need to Remember About My Audience?

- People are out there searching for my talent, knowledge, and the solutions that I can provide;
- They deserve to hear my expertise;
- I have multiple ways to get my message to them.

Lastly, remember your "why" and why you're putting yourself out there. Yes, it's to become better known, to showcase your expertise, to grow your business—and most importantly, to *help* people! You got into your specialty because you believe that everyone should have access to great ideas. And the content you offer to the media can put your knowledge into the hands of more people so that they can enhance their lives. Your expertise could easily be the answer to their needs.

All of the previous information will pull together your business mantra, something you can say to yourself whenever those "I'm not worthy" gremlins enter your mind. And now that you have the skill set, and your mantra, I hope that you feel empowered to start soliciting ways to be seen, heard, and known for your unique genius.

Where to Begin

Get out there and do the thing you know you must! You'll feel so much better to have taken action. And we, your audience, will be better off having heard from you. I cannot wait to see you shine!

I always love hearing from anyone implementing my strategies, so please get in touch. Send me your pitch, and I'll give you my honest opinion and suggestions if any to improve it. Reach me at amanda@amandaberlin.com.

The three designers I'd like to share with you are Erika Ward, Rachel Moriarty, and Wendy Woloshchuk. Although there are dozens of designers that come to my mind, I chose these three because in the nearly five years of the podcast, I have watched these designers literally grow their visibility exponentially.

What Do I Need to Remember About the Decision-Maker?

Erika Ward is the most known of the three designers, especially back in 2016, when I met each of these ladies. In fact, I discovered Erika before I launched the podcast. Her name appears on my very first wish list of potential podcast guests. I still have that list!

In the fall of 2015, as part of my podcast launch plan, I Googled endlessly both on the Net and on Instagram for potential guests: Top 10 interior designers in Los Angeles, in Boston, in Atlanta, top 10 modern interior designers, top 10 luxury interior designers—you name it, I searched it. Erika's name came up in that Atlanta search, and the more I learned about her, the more I wanted her on the show. I poured over her blog, which according to my notes was then called Blue Label Bungalow although is now titled Behind the Curtain. Erika taught design tips. She shared details about herself, her family, her clients, and her projects. As widely known, published, and accomplished as Erika was when I found her and met her, her visibility has skyrocketed in the last five years. Her Instagram following in October 2015 was, to be exact, 7,732. Now, in summer 2020, she has grown it to 37,600! A visit to her website today is a veritable who's who of her press in design publications and media collaborations.

Amanda is 100 percent correct: Decision-makers have a job to do. They need engaging, interesting, relevant content day in and day out. You have a job to do too. Show up, create content, state your point of view on design, on life, on whatever matters to you. This will be different for each of us; it is ours and ours alone. The key is to share it, to let the world know, to give the publishers, the TV producers, the podcasters some reason to look to you as the expert, as a resource, as an esteemed business owner.

To learn more about how Erika built her business, go back and listen to her podcast episode #6.

What Do I Need to Remember About My Audience?

When I met Rachel Moriarty, if I remember correctly, after 10 years as a full-time advisor for high net worth individuals and side hustling as a designer, she would stake her claim as a full-time designer in only a few months after we met. A very early listener and supporter of my podcast, she caught my attention. Vibrant, beautiful, and determined are the adjectives that came to mind, then and now.

Do you know what I noticed about Rachel Moriarty?

She remembered her audience. She remembered some people love color, just like she does. Despite launching her full-time firm at the height of the industry's deep dive into all things white, gray, and neutral, Rachel knew there are people like she is—people who are not middle of the road about color, in their lives or in their homes. So, contrary to every other photo on Instagram, Rachel donned beautiful, exotic, colorful scarves and started attracting potential clients by talking to them and giving them permission to design with color. She shared how creating boldly designed, color-filled spaces brought her joy and happiness. It worked. Her audience found her, they loved her, and they hired her to design their homes.

Do you. Be you. Show up as you in all that you do in your business. You don't need the entire possible audience of design enthusiasts to build a profitable business; you need only the ones who value your skill, your talent, and love your style.

Rachel shared her own advice on the podcast, episode #55. I recommend you listen. Then in episode #274, I shared how I watched Rachel build a robust pipeline from literally nothing by being brave, decisive, and committed to visibility. If you haven't heard this story about Rachel, you're in for a treat.

What Do I Need to Remember About Myself?

Wendy Woloshchuk remembered that everything she knew about design was enough. Wendy began a consumer FB live show called *The Daily Details*, and she remembered "I know my stuff." Each week, with her bright, outgoing personality, Wendy taught consumers how to style a coffee table, how to select lighting, even how to take care of plants! I remember this one because as I flipped through FB one day I stopped to watch because I needed to know how to care for, of all plants, a philodendron—famous for being one of the easiest of all house plants to care for. To Amanda's point, however, even the simplest of things you know can be mind-blowing for someone else...or in this case, at minimum, quite useful!

Today, Wendy has thousands of followers on her Facebook page, "Details Full Service Interiors," and she has been recognized by consumers while shopping at Home Goods and Target. Wendy, along with Marianne Cherico and Debbe Daley, now leads an awesome group whose mission it is to help designers be better business owners and better designers. Their group is called "Design for Today Collaborative." I encourage you to connect with them.

It all begins with you and in having a point of view. It continues with content creation, in whatever form that takes, Facebook, Instagram, blogging, podcasting. The results are earned by delivering quality and consistency. Take Amanda's advice. Work through her exercises. As you uncover your stories and your passions, it will all begin to piece together and make sense.

Public relations is for you, in your very own pond. When you understand it and leverage it, it can make a big impact on your business.

–LN

About the Author

After more than a decade in the New York City public relations world, Amanda Berlin now uses her pitch powers for good. She helps entrepreneurs step into their presence, create a story that inspires others, and spread their message in the media. Amanda has created a library of template guides and trainings and works one-on-one with clients to guide them to strategic story-telling and media relations based on her 12 years of experience guiding strategy for major brands in the corporate world. Amanda and her clients have been featured in all types of media—from *Business Insider* to *Entrepreneur on Fire* and from WNYW Fox 5 to Bustle. com. She's the host of *The Empowered Publicity* podcast and loves arming soul-powered business owners with the ideas and skill set they need to go from hidden industry gem to recognizable trusted expert. Amanda has spoken on the topics of visibility, publicity, and entrepreneurship at BizChix Live, Style Collective Raleigh and New York City, Body Local, Hoboken Entrepreneur Group, and more.

Amanda Berlin has been a featured guest on A *Well-Designed Business*® podcast episodes 420 and 571.

Section Four

Becoming the CEO

CHAPTER 7

Amber De La Garza

It is not easy being an entrepreneur. It takes a ton of courage, a ton of energy, and a ton of passion. I'll bet you have friends, just like I do, who have told you how lucky you are to own your business. You have heard it, "You can do what you want, when you want, take a day off whenever you want, **you are so lucky**." You've smiled and thought to yourself, "Yup, I can do whatever I want. I can put my kids to bed and go back to work until midnight. I can steal afternoons from our vacation to review client proposals. I can work straight through weekends so often that Tuesdays no longer feel any different than Sundays. Yup, living the life, that's me."

Am I right?

Amber knows that. Amber coaches and helps people just like us get our life back. She helps us get back to the real reasons we became our own bosses in the first place—so we can build a company, a life, a body of work that fulfills us and creates joy in our life...a business that actually gives us exactly what all of our friends think we have, which is the ability to live life on **our** terms.

If this sounds impossible, read on. Amber is about to change your life. The good news is it is not about spreadsheets and high-tech tools, so if military organization is not your jam, don't worry. This is about changing your beliefs. This is about how we think and how we approach productivity. You have heard me say it dozens of times: Our biggest problem is usually right between our own ears. Often, we make the mistake of looking outside ourselves for reasons we are unsuccessful rather than looking at our own thoughts, habits, and actions. We placate ourselves and rationalize with stories like:

- *If I only had enough help, I could work a normal week.*
- *If I only had more time, I could create an organized business.*

*How we think about things, how we process thoughts and ideas, dramatically affects how we show up in our life and in our business. Here is the plain and simple truth: The above statements are not facts. They are limiting beliefs. They are the stories **between our ears**—external factors that ultimately have little to no effect on our ability to be successful. To be successful and profitable, we must begin by letting go of the stories which we have clung to and have sabotaged our business.*

So be prepared. Amber is going to teach us something much larger, much more valuable than how to set up a to-do list.

-LN

Leverage the Productive Activities Driving Your Profits

Amber De La Garza

Before you ventured out as a business owner, you no doubt dreamed of living out your passion being creative and designing beautiful spaces for your clients and of the freedom you'd have creating your own schedule. Instead, you are inundated with behind-the-scenes work, leaving little to no time for yourself, and often feel chained to your business like a prisoner, despite loving what you do. You use your nights and weekends to get caught up on all the designs and uncanny number of emails demanding your attention, leaving little time for family and friends. You like the idea of taking on more clients so you can become more profitable and create a better life for yourself and your family, but you're too stuck in the mud of daily operations to execute on growing your business. You're constantly being pulled in numerous directions by employees, vendors, clients, and contractors, and it's wearing you out! You're overwhelmed, exhausted, constantly out of time, and starting to wonder if being a business owner is really for you.

The truth is that you're fully capable of running a profitable business that doesn't steal all your free time and energy from the people and things you love. You're fully capable of doing what it takes to grow your business while running daily operations smoothly. You're fully capable of managing your time effectively so that you end each day being completely satisfied with the great amount and scope of work you accomplished. You're fully capable; you're just not equipped. You're not equipped with the productivity "know-how" to be increasingly profitable without being constantly overwhelmed and run down. It's time to add true productivity to your tool bag.

The Truth About Productivity

The Lies

So here's the thing about productivity...it's become a buzzword over the years, and as such, numerous variations of its meaning exist and a lot of myths have gained traction. Despite what some other experts may have you believe, productivity is not all about being organized. Otherwise, all the super-organized people you know with clean desks, neat, short stacks of paper, and everything in its place would be highly productive. In many cases, those super-organized people are not productive at all because they spend far too much of their valuable time organizing instead of working on their high-value activities that generate revenue.

Productivity is also not all about being efficient because you could be incredibly efficient doing administrative and useless tasks that have little to no effect on your revenue and still get no closer to reaching your goals. There's no question that being organized and efficient can support your productivity. If you're able to work through your tasks quickly and don't need to waste time and energy searching for lost keys, wallets, papers, and files, you have more time to invest in your high-value activities. Efficiency and organization are not the same as productivity, however.

Finally, productivity is not about getting everything done. That feat would be impossible. Even thinking you can get everything done is counterproductive and creates an unnecessary sense of being overwhelmed. The sooner you reconcile with the truth that you will never get it all done, the better off you will be because you will be forced to prioritize and focus your time and energy on your most important tasks and projects. Productivity is about doing the right things, not everything.

The Truth

So what exactly is productivity then? Productivity is simply **investing your best time into your best activities**, with your best time being blocks of focused, uninterrupted time, and your best activities being the high-value activities that get you closer to achieving your goals. Counter to popular belief, productivity is not an inherited gene. It is a skill you can learn and hone, then the choice to use that skill must be made consistently every day. Choose to be productive daily, and the positive effects will ripple throughout every nook and cranny of your business, especially your profitability. All it takes is choosing to consistently invest your best time into your best activities.

Identify Your Best Time

All time is not created equal. If it was, you'd have no problem banging out your best work at 3:00 a.m. While night owls may prosper in the wee hours, most people function better in the daytime. Simply working during the day does not make you productive, though. To be productive, you must work during your best times—the times when you can most easily get in your focused zone and work uninterrupted, with minimal distractions. You have to be true to your unique circadian rhythms and to those times when your energy and ability to focus are naturally at their highest. If you have a hard time keeping your eyes open two hours after lunch, that is hardly the best time to tackle your most important work requiring your utmost focus.

Even if you're acutely aware that your energy peaks between 9:00 and 11:00 a.m., your environment during those hours may still prevent you from focusing on your high-value activities. For example, you might have vendors calling you, employees interrupting you, or kids playing loudly in the next room during those morning hours. Your best time is a combination of the time of day when you are mentally and physically at your best *along with* the environment that best supports your productivity. The key is tuning into your circadian rhythms while simultaneously working in an optimized environment.

Ask yourself: Are you able to focus better when it's warm? Cold? When it's light? Dark? Quiet? Noisy? Some business owners prefer the quiet of their office with the door closed to work on their detailed design projects, while others prefer the noise of a bustling coffee shop, packed with people. Do you focus best with soft music playing? A sound machine? The ticking of a clock? Do essential oils help you focus? Do you work better standing up, sitting down on a chair, or bouncing on a ball? Although often disregarded, all of those environmental factors have an effect on your mood, focus, energy, and ability to do your best work. You must know what environment best supports your productivity so that you can create it and utilize it wisely during your periods of naturally high energy and focus. Give yourself permission to see what works, then lean into it whenever you aim to be productive.

The following resource will help you determine your best work environment: www.TheProductivitySpecialist.com/LuAnn

Identify Your Best Activities

You're not meant to be productive all day, every day. You would burn out even trying to accomplish that impossible feat over the long haul. Your business needs you to be productive daily, however. To do so, you must intentionally invest your time in the right activities that will grow your business and increase your profitability, but not just during any time—during your best time. Investing your best time into working on your high-value activities is being productive, and it's exactly the "magic" that will make your business profitable. When you're not clear on what your high-value activities are, everything seems equally important. How many times have you found yourself glancing up at the clock and becoming bewildered by how you just spent three hours in your inbox or scrolling through Instagram with little to show for it?

As the owner of your interior design business, you are directly responsible for determining what it will take to improve your productivity so that you can become more effective and see your profitability radically increase. No matter what your goals are, being profitable should be #1. Profitability ensures that you can stay in business and continue helping people by serving the world with your talents and expertise. Higher profits enable you to make a bigger impact on your life, your family, your community, and those you serve. Your profitability provides job security for those who work for you and security for their families, as well as for your own. Being your own boss is a good thing. Being profitable? A fabulous one!

It is rare to find an unproductive person running a highly profitable business or a productive person running an unprofitable business. Productivity and profit go hand in hand. It's imperative, then, to improve your productivity to increase your profitability.

As a business owner, you have chosen to live a life by design. Undoubtedly, you want freedom and flexibility, both with your time and your finances, but consider this: Are you doing everything it takes to excel so that you can remain a business owner and continue creating your own schedule and rules? You might just be passively going through the motions of being a business owner each day, spending too much time doing administrative tasks, managing employees, and putting out fires. Has your profitability plateaued but your expenses increased as vendors keep raising their prices and inflation takes its toll? If you don't improve your productivity, you might be only a few canceled projects away from going out of business.

The fact is your time is finite. You cannot create more, buy more, barter for more, or wave a magic wand to get more time. Time is always referred to as your most precious resource for a reason. You simply cannot continue keeping yourself busy with activities that are not bringing you closer to your goals and vision of success. If you want to stay in business and grow your business, you need to run a profitable business. That starts with choosing to be productive on a consistent basis by proactively investing your best time into your best activities consistently.

Your High-Value Activity Buckets

After nearly a decade coaching, training, and working with hundreds of small-business owners to improve their productivity, I have narrowed down the overarching, highly productive activities on which small-business owners need to be hyper-focusing their time and energy to increase profitability: Marketing/visibility, sales, servicing clients, and leadership. I call them the four *High-Value Activity Buckets*.

Marketing/Visibility

The *Marketing/Visibility* bucket is the beginning of your profitability pipeline. It includes the various activities in which you can engage to let people know who you are and how you can help them. How do people find out about you? How do they know what you do? How do they know your interior design firm even exists? How do you make sure your name comes to mind when they want to redesign the entire first floor of their house in the Hamptons? Social media, podcast interviews, websites, blog articles, regular value-added emails, social events, strategic referral partners, and feature spots in a magazine are a few ways you can strategically market your business and increase your visibility. Find the two or three strategies that work best to market your business, and double down on those to stay visible to your past clients and become visible to potential clients. If you're failing to consistently focus on marketing and visibility, you likely will not have enough sales conversations to sustain your profitability. One flows into the other. Successful marketing efforts will lead to more and more revenue-generating sales conversations.

Sales

The next bucket in which to invest your time is the *Sales* bucket. Sales activities include all the discovery calls, consultations, proposals, presentations, contract negotiations, and follow-up activities leading to you closing the deal. It's not enough for people to know about you. They need to want to do business with you, trust in your expertise, and be sold on the vision you present to them. Those ingredients don't mix well if your sales skills are subpar and you botch the presentation. Fine-tune your presentation and sales skills to achieve higher conversion rates. When your marketing efforts are working, you will have an influx of people coming to you for sales conversations, but you are the one who must convincingly share how you can best serve them, meet their needs, and exceed their expectations. If you don't have enough sales conversations or tend to botch the ones you do have, you certainly will not take on enough clients to stay in business for the long haul. On the other hand, successful sales conversations will lead to servicing a growing number of clients and increased profitability.

Servicing Clients

It is also important to spend your time in the *Servicing Clients* bucket. Servicing clients includes performing such activities as selecting color palettes and fabrics, creating designs, presenting them to clients, coordinating with contractors, subcontractors, architects, and engineers, purchasing furniture, accessories, and art, and doing walk-throughs. While those areas are likely your favorite activities in the scope of your work and the reason why you entered the interior design industry to begin with, I caution you not to indulge in the temptation to spend all your time in the *Servicing Clients* bucket. Allowing your time there to expand exponentially because it's enjoyable robs other *High-Value Activity Buckets.* Don't service your clients at the expense of failing to show up in the *Marketing/Visibility* and *Sales* buckets. You must keep your profitability pipeline flowing by consistently investing in your marketing/visibility and sales activities, otherwise you will not have a continuous flow of clients to serve.

Good judgment within each area is also extremely important. Just because an activity technically falls under the category of marketing/visibility, sales, or servicing clients, doesn't mean it necessarily falls into one of your *High-Value Activity Buckets.* Sure, building a new, user-friendly, SEO-focused website with an elegant theme that speaks to wealthy homeowners may increase your visibility, thus making it a marketing activity, but unless you have a background in web design, building out your site is likely not the best use of your time and energy and therefore not one of your high-value activities. If an activity lies outside your zone of genius, or if it makes financial or logical sense for someone else to do it, delegate that activity and save your time for the high-value activities that only you can do. Also, as your business evolves over time and your roles change, the activities in each bucket will change because you'll be able to niche down into the exact, productive activities that you should be doing and outsource more tasks and projects.

Leadership

Leadership is the final bucket, and as you scale your business, that bucket becomes more important. If you are in business, you are in the business of leading others. It doesn't matter if you are delegating tasks to your assistant, building a small team, growing a large team, or working solely with independent contractors for one-off, specialized projects. No one achieves their dreams entirely on their own. Fill your time and talent gaps by relying on the time and talents of others. Make sure your team feels supported and has the information, skills, and resources to carry out their tasks and execute your vision with confidence. Meet with them on a regular basis to address their needs and concerns. That time is never wasted if it's used intentionally to pave the way forward. When you take time to invest in and lead your team, you are ultimately investing in the success of your business.

As your business grows and evolves, you will be investing much more of your time naturally into the *Leadership* bucket and less time in your other three *High-Value Activity Buckets*. That transition happens almost seamlessly because as your profitability increases, you will be able to hire additional support and delegate responsibilities previously reserved for yourself. Instead of being the CEO, janitor, and everything in between, you will be leading teams who are executing the activities in your other *High-Value Activity Buckets*. Every hour that your team spends working in the *Marketing/Visibility*, *Sales*, and *Servicing Clients* buckets is an hour you can reclaim for the high-value activities that only you can do to grow your business, as well as for your passions, hobbies, friends, and family.

The Other Bucket

If you feel out of time, overwhelmed, and overcommitted running your business, you're likely spending too much time in a fifth undesirable *Other* bucket. As world-renowned entrepreneur Jim Rohn said, "Time is our most valuable asset, yet we tend to waste it, kill it, and spend it rather than invest it." The *Other* bucket is home to all the low-value activities in which you engage that are not specifically revenue-generating—tasks like answering the phone, checking emails, reconciling expenses, paying taxes, and (ahem) scrolling social media. True, many of the tasks in the *Other* bucket are important and even necessary, but they are not where you should be spending the majority of your time. You've likely heard the quip, "You're too busy working in your business to work on your business." You're wasting, killing, and spending your time, as Jim Rohn said, rather than investing it in the high-value activities that provide a solid return.

You may start off each day with the best intention of *I'm going to get this project done and make major headway on that one*, but then get stuck in your email inbox, returning vendor phone calls, and editing contracts. Are you doing your own bookkeeping? Answering your phone? Posting to your social media accounts?

Perhaps you find yourself endlessly scrolling there as the minute hand keeps making revolutions. What activities are keeping you busy all day long, so that you're not investing time in your *Marketing/Visibility*, *Sales*, *Servicing Clients*, and *Leadership* buckets? It's those *Other* bucket activities that leave you exhausted at the end of each day with little to show for it. On the other hand, working in your four *High-Value Activity Buckets* will keep you on track toward your goals, feeling accomplished, and more profitable.

It doesn't matter if you choose to work 30 hours a week or 60. There's only so much time in a day, and every minute you spend working in the *Other* bucket is a minute that you could be spending in the *Marketing/Visibility*, *Sales*, *Servicing Clients*, or *Leadership* buckets. Identify the "opportunity cost" of each instance that you slip your hand into the *Other* bucket. Decrease your time spent there, and you will reclaim loads of time for the revenue-generating activities that keep your business floating higher up in the black.

Your mindset is also negatively impacted when you spend too much time in the *Other* bucket. Think back to a day that you were super-productive. Maybe you signed a couple of new clients after stellar presentations or wrapped up a large-scale design project with the best possible outcome. You went home feeling amazing about yourself, your business, and the impact you're making in the world. Your mindset was fantastic! Then recall and compare the many more days where you went home exhausted and zonked out as soon as your head hit the pillow, or you could not fall asleep because you could not stop thinking about your endless list of to-dos, none of which you managed to accomplish that day. When "busy" days as opposed to productive days are your norm, it affects your entrepreneurial mindset. You start doubting yourself and don't show up in the world as consistently as you would like. You don't go after the next big marketing opportunity. You don't ask for the sale. You don't service your clients in the way you would if you had a positive mindset. It is of the utmost priority that you protect your mindset. Choosing to be productive every day will help you to protect your mindset and build the confidence to continue doing what it takes to show up and level up your business.

As unacceptable as spending time in the *Other* bucket may sound, it is not to be dismissed. Administrative and housekeeping tasks still need to be taken care of unless you're able to jet-set all over the world while your company practically runs itself. If so, good for you! If not and you're still grinding day-to-day, you're still dipping your hand too much into the *Other* bucket. The key is in viewing your time as the precious resource it is and as an investment in the success (*or failure*) of your business. If you live in the *Other* bucket, you'll reap the seeds you sowed there. You'll have a trophy case full of menial tasks marked *completed*, but minimal profits to show for it. Do your necessary *Other* bucket tasks efficiently and effectively, then get out!

If you constantly find yourself exhausted at the end of each day and are unsure how you spent yesterday or even today, that's a problem. You should be able to review your day at the end of it and feel like you conquered it because you tackled high-value activities that will make a major impact in your business. You did the marketing that it takes for people to discover you and feel an immediate connection to your work. You closed the deal on a $100,000 chain restaurant renovation with the potential of adding more locations. You made your clients' mouths drop in gleeful astonishment when they saw their finished basement, complete with that surprise, one-of-a-kind chest from France that they had their eye on. You delegated numerous tasks to your employees because you empowered them and trusted in their ability to execute them effectively. Run your business so that you feel you won the day every day! Proactively invest in your *Marketing/ Visibility*, *Sales*, *Servicing Clients*, and *Leadership* buckets, while just dipping your hand briefly in the *Other* bucket.

The following resource will help you determine your high-value activities: www.TheProductivitySpecialist.com/LuAnn

I started my business because I witnessed too many talented and passionate small-business owners around me burning out. They knew how they wanted to serve people and had the passion and drive to carry it out, but they lacked personal productivity skills, which left them spending too much time in the *Other* bucket, stressed out, overwhelmed, out of financial resources, and throwing in the towel. By not improving their productivity to increase their profitability, they cheated themselves out of the freedom and flexibility of running their own business and cheated the world out of everything they had to offer. Imagine how different the interior design world would be if Elsie de Wolfe, David Rockwell, and Kelly Wearstler went back to nine to five jobs early on because their businesses fell prey to them living in the *Other* bucket.

Consistently productive business owners become profitable, grow really fast, and succeed in the interior design space. They take control of their future by investing their time in the activities that provide the greatest return. I guarantee that you will not experience the greatest returns in your inbox, scrolling Instagram, organizing your office, perusing other designers' websites, or consuming interior design podcasts until your brain is numb. You will score the greatest returns when you strategically and intentionally spend your time on the revenue-generating activities that only you can do. And when you do so, you'll be more efficient and find even more time for those high-value, money-making activities.

Mind blown, am I right?

If not, please, sit with what Amber is saying. Take it in. To really reap the benefits of her advice, you have to stretch and reach for the mindset shift. Intellectually, we all know what busywork is, but when we are doing it, we rationalize that it is productivity. Think about the high-value activity buckets Amber is describing. Think about intentionally working in each. This is not the same as spending a day being busy.

I know all the best business practices, such as work in your super power and to time-block your days, weeks, months. I also remember my friend, Madeleine MacRae, taught us to identify the $10, the $100, the $1,000, and $10,000 an hour activities. She explained, as the CEO you are to spend most of your time in that $10,000 an hour zone. And there I was, banging my head against a wall, because I knew I was spending hours in the wrong activities. Since I wasn't ready to make another hire, I thought I had no choice...until I hired Amber to coach me.

My major mindset shift was in how I do the $10, $100, and $1,000 an hour activities. Amber drilled into me the goal was not to simply complete the low-value activities; instead, the goal was to intentionally manage them.

She asked me, "LuAnn, where do you lose the most time? What prevents you from doing your high-value activities?" My immediate response, "Email."

I had come to truly hate email. So much so that I disconnected email from my phone in the summer of 2019, and yes, it is still disconnected. I complained, however, that wasn't enough. It still overwhelmed me. She said, "You have an assistant, why don't we task her with all email?" My response, "No way. I get emails from potential sponsors, **I have to answer those**. I get emails from PR reps pitching their clients, **I have to vet those**. I get heartfelt emails from my listeners, **I have to be the one to answer those**. The beast, otherwise known as email, was a colossal time-suck every, darn, day.

Do know what life-changing fix Amber came up with?

Lisa, my assistant would:

1. Create folders in my inbox:

    *   Sponsor inquiries
    *   Listener email
    *   Pitches to be on my show
    *   Priority, time-sensitive, need action
    *   To be done—whenever

    2. Lisa would read all emails, take care of anything she could, and distribute the rest into the folders.

Wait for the magic . . .

    3. Lisa would schedule, every week, time blocks in my calendar for me to address each folder.

*   Lu: Handle priority-action items;
*   Lu: Answer listener emails;
*   Lu: Vet podcast pitches;
*   Lu: Respond to sponsor inquiries;

- *Lu: Clean up whenever items.*

An hour here, a half-hour there, throughout the week. No more opening email and coming up for air hours later. Because I know time is in the schedule, I can ignore emails when I am supposed to be working in a high-value activity bucket!

OMG. It was genius!

Was it easy?

No ma'am, no sir. You know me...I know processes and systems are crucial, but personally, I resist them. Actually, I mean, **I actively resist them.** I am a big thinker, a dreamer, a visionary, a strategist. I know I need systems, but for me it's like I know I should choose broccoli over French fries. I want the French fries, but because I know what's better for me, I choose broccoli. I like the results when I make good choices. So, I have learned to **"mostly"** choose systems and broccoli, no matter how tasty those salty, crispy fries are.

It is no joke to say Amber had her work cut out with me. But the lights finally went on when I understood the difference between being busy and being productive. Change is not easy, and I, too, am a work in progress, but if your desire for a different outcome is great enough or the pain you are in is great enough, you can change. There is a work-around for anything that holds you back from being your most productive self. Place a priority on figuring out how to spend the most time in your highest-value buckets and bask in the reward of your hard work.

-LN

About the Author

Amber De La Garza is The Productivity Specialist! Amber is a sought-after coach, trainer, speaker, writer, host of the *Productivity Straight Talk* podcast, and creator of S.T.O.P. Leverage Formula. She works with driven entrepreneurs to execute actionable solutions to maximize profits, reduce stress, and make time for what matters most!

Amber De La Garza has been a featured guest on *A Well-Designed Business®* podcast episodes 385 and 577.

CHAPTER 8

Desi Creswell

T hank you, Sarah Montgomery. Thank you, my friend, for introducing me to Desi Creswell.

In our very first phone call, I connected with Desi. As she explained her point of view on life, on business, and on success, I kept thinking and saying, "Yes, I agree. Yes, that is so true." I remember telling her, "When you talk about your work, I hear the how and why of my own thoughts and beliefs about achieving success in work." What to me were feelings actually were instincts—assimilated for years—being explained in practical terms. It was kind of crazy.

You know me. You know I was raised on woo. Back in the 70s, we didn't call it woo. We called it positive thinking, we called it visualization, we called it creating and achieving your goals. Between my mom, my Aunt Honey, Og Mandino, Wayne Dwyer, Napoleon Hill, James Allen, Zig Ziglar, Dale Carnegie, Leo Buscaglia, and then later, Tony Robbins and Oprah, I no longer remember who taught me what, but I am grateful for every one of them and their influence on my life.

I started reading the works of these icons at 10 years old. I read, I believed, I absorbed, I lived. It worked. That was enough for me. Now Desi was reminding me of the reasons and the principles of why woo works.

To grasp this feeling that I experienced in that first conversation with Desi, think of it this way. We all have a friend or a client who completely misses the mark when choosing colors. But you, you have a knack for selecting color for paint, fabric, tile—all of it. You don't remember why or how you learned this, but you know when a color is right. You see a stone wall with various shades, and you can nail the right paint color to enhance and coordinate with it. So, you go along for years, aware you can do this, but never giving much thought as to why some colors go with others. They just do.

Then, you take a color science course, or you read about color theory. You learn about the color wheel and all the reasons why certain colors coordinate or contrast with others. And you think, instinctively, "I understood what color to choose, and here it is, in a practical guide, why which color should be chosen." Somewhere along the line, you learned it. Not in one place...rather, every place, at the same time.

Desi's chapter is the color wheel for knowing the how and why of creating a life and a business you enjoy. She breaks it down so it makes sense. And she challenges you to think deeply about what you want and what you are willing to do to create it.

This, I love.

-LN

Creating Your Ideal Life and Business
Desi Creswell

Getting Started

Right now, I probably can tell you what your to-do list looks like. It's overloaded with miscellaneous tasks, project deadlines, and notes to self for "someday." But what it likely doesn't include is the time to plan for intentionally creating your *dream* business. You are not alone. Most, if not all of us, have big goals but never enough time or focus to decide—let alone, execute—what we really want for ourselves. I understand how it feels to be overwhelmed by all of it because I, too, was frustrated with my reality not meshing with the idea that I could have it all. But I learned how to create a fulfilling life and business where the two support each other—and you can too. The information and examples I share here speak to interior designers because that is who I serve, but it applies to any business owner who wants to tune into both areas of life. Read on.

In the marketing world, we hear so much about defining our ideal client. While I completely agree that step is important, what often gets left out of the process is defining our very own ideal business—one that aligns with our values, priorities, and the life we want to create. If you are like I am, you likely started your own interior design business because you wanted to have the freedom, flexibility, and income potential that is available through entrepreneurship. But in the process of serving clients, meeting deadlines, and wearing all of the hats, we can easily lose sight of the big picture, get caught in the motions, and the day-to-day begins to feel like a burden. Then, we tell ourselves that we are too busy to step back and intentionally define what we want for ourselves personally and professionally. When we do not make new decisions, we repeat the past and limit ourselves.

Throughout the following pages, I will show you how to create what I call an "Aligned Business." We will start first by defining what an aligned business is and what it means to you. I do not believe in a one-size-fits-all approach to building a business, so this starting point is your chance to take a look at what you specifically want to create for yourself. We will also discuss how to create a life and business vision and identify top priorities that will act as guideposts to inform all of your decisions moving forward.

Now is your opportunity to pause, grab a notebook, your favorite beverage, and make space for these exercises. While slowing down seems counterintuitive when we are constantly told to speed up, the decisions you make during this time will set you up for creating new results and seeing what is truly possible for you. Together, we will create a roadmap toward your aligned business. Whether you are just starting out or you've been at it for a while, this work will transform the way you approach your work. You are going to love it. Let's dive in.

To gain the most from the following exercises I encourage you to pause and write out your answers as you move through the chapter. The knowledge this chapter provides, plus implementation by you, is where your transformation will occur. To assist you in this process I have created a custom journal where you can record your insights.

Visit www.desicreswell.com/luann3 to download and print your free copy.

What Is an Aligned Business?

An aligned business is one that supports and enhances your life rather than letting the business run your life. When you have an aligned business, you do less but do it better because you are intentional about your core service offerings, design fees, and where you spend your energy and focus. You have a greater sense of fulfillment, purpose, and meaning because daily decisions are built upon choices that serve your personal version and vision of success.

An aligned business gives you permission to do business *your* way. It's serving the type of clients with whom you love to work, and it's setting up a studio that allows for the type of growth, profit, and flexibility that you desire. There are countless ways to build a design practice, so it's up to you to decide how you want to run yours. It comes down to choosing what you want your business to look like. If you don't define and implement what you want, outside forces will define your business for you. This leads to overwhelm and feelings of dissatisfaction, even if the business looks outwardly "successful."

Why Do You Need a Business **and** Life Vision?

We got into the design industry because we love the work. We are excited to take on *any* project that comes our way, and at first, taking on any job isn't necessarily a problem. But as we continue to develop and grow, our business can start to take on a life of its own. Without setting the course, you are likely to end up in a place that you never meant to go. That trajectory is why defining your business *and* life vision is the first step toward building an aligned business. Your unique vision becomes the foundation for the type of business you want most, while also supporting success in all areas of your life. If we don't intentionally make choices that support a desired outcome, we end up frustrated, working late nights and weekends, taking on projects that aren't a good fit because we are used to helping anyone and everyone, and feeling like the business is our own task master instead of serving the life we want to live.

I want you to picture a boat in the middle of the ocean. The boat is your business, and the waves are the incoming influences such as clients, projects, vendors, and tradespeople. A boat in the water, even one with an anchor, is never stationary. There always is movement.

As the waves come and go, the boat is pushed and pulled in many directions. The same is true of your business. Creating a life and business vision that is specific to you is the difference between letting the currents take you where they will versus picking up a pair of oars and starting to row. So how do we set and stay on course?

When considering your ideal business, it's important to look at it through two lenses: (1) the CEO with big dreams and goals, and (2) the human behind it all. It is common to want to silo our business, but it is a fallacy that our business operates in a vacuum. Generally speaking, how we do one thing is how we do everything, so to assume that your business is an entity separate from the rest of your life will not serve you in the long run.

To be clear, when I talk about an aligned business, I am not talking about work-life balance. In fact, the term "balance" perpetuates the idea that work and life should be separate and split evenly at that. I believe that the two are interconnected and that everyone's particular blend will look different. Some blends will place more emphasis on the work, and some will place more emphasis on the life. And here's the best part: it's all amazing.

What is most important as you create your vision is that you love *your* reasons behind *your* vision. It's not about how anyone else is doing it. It's about how *you* want to do it.

It Must Be Compelling to You

As you move toward an aligned business, you must also define what success means to you. There are many ways to build a successful design practice. If your definition doesn't match the status quo, yet you continue to pursue that path because everyone else does it that way, you'll always feel out of alignment. Taking the time to create your own vision based on your own values is much more compelling. And when you connect with your "why" in a compelling way, you are more motivated to make it happen.

Now is the time to define what success looks like to you and why that version of success is so important to you. Take a few moments to write out your answers to the following prompts.

How do you define success? Is it reaching a certain income level, having high-profile clients, being published in magazines, ending the day before the kids are out of school?

What is your "why?" Why will you continue to work toward your vision until it is reached, no matter what?

Is your "why" compelling enough for you to start taking action? Why or why not?

What would make your "why" even more compelling?

Often, when we start to dream of what we really desire, our tendency is to scale back to comfort. We worry that what we really want is not possible for us. The idea might feel too unrealistic, or you might be afraid of the disappointment if the vision is not attained. Retreating to a sense of security is human nature.

Putting aside those fears for a moment, if you thought of yourself as someone else (one who is more successful, more deserving, more business savvy, etc.), would your vision be even bigger? What came to mind for you? Is there something more? Give yourself the gift of the truth and write down anything that came up but felt too big. What if you are wrong about your capabilities?

Belief in Yourself

So many of my clients get caught in the "how-to" stage. They want to know the specific steps that they need to take and are looking for the *exact* blueprint. The underlying belief here is that if they just figure out the right way to do things, if they get the right system, marketing plan or social media strategy, then success is guaranteed. In the coming chapters, you'll learn some of the best practices and strategies from fellow experts. Before you dive into the exact "how to," however, you must first believe that you are capable.

Belief in your ability to create an aligned business is what will ultimately create your fulfilled vision. We are taught to believe that all we need is our actions in order to create results, but the reality is that we must first believe in our own possibility. With belief, we generate positive emotions, such as inspired, committed, determined, or motivated. Our beliefs create our feelings, which fuel our actions, which then produce our results. What we believe is what we create.

A belief is simply a thought you have had so many times that you have accepted it as true. Throughout our lives, we adopt beliefs directly and indirectly. They can come from your family or origin, cultural and societal norms, and from our own observations about how the world around us works. Most of the time, our beliefs are so ingrained that we may not even be aware of them. Or they may feel like a collection of facts that reflects our life story or who we are as a person. Some beliefs serve us well, while others hold us back. Awareness is key. Once you have an understanding of your current belief system, you can consciously decide if you would like to keep those beliefs.

Let's explore how your current beliefs show up in your life. Consider a result that you would like in your life or business that you have yet to create, and answer the following questions.

What do you believe about your ability to create what you want in your life or business?

Who would you be without this belief?

Without this belief, what actions would you take to create your desired result?

Are you willing to be wrong about yourself in order to create a new result?

Values and Priorities

In order to shift into an aligned business, assessing and defining your values and priorities becomes very important. Our values are principles that provide us with a guiding foundation for who we want to be and how we want to show up in the world. Our values are a small set of essential and timeless principles. Examples include connection, leadership, kindness, growth, simplicity, perseverance, and openness.

What are your top five values? Next to each, write down one way that you currently embody this value.

Priorities are more fluid over the course of your career and may change year to year. They are activities, practices, relationships, and results that are important to you. Examples could include doubling your revenue in one year, being featured in a national publication, or leaving the office early two days per week.

In essence, our time and energy are like currency. Some priorities may take more time and energy; others less. We have a fixed amount at any given time. So, where do you want to spend yours? Are you spending your time, energy, and attention on tasks that support your present priorities?

Let's assess your current priorities and how you spend your time. Take a few moments to complete the following exercise.

Make a list of your top five priorities in order.

Why did you rank them in this order? What stands out to you about your #1 priority?

Think about how you spent your day yesterday. Did the way you spend your time reflect the order of these priorities?

Does anything need to change about your priorities to better align with your life and business vision? What?

No one priority is innately superior to another. The objective of the above exercise is simply a matter of getting clear for your own benefit. With clarity, you can start to tie your daily activities back to each priority on the list, making your actions more meaningful and effective.

We are faced with daily choices that either move us toward or away from our goals. And more often than not, we are asking ourselves to choose what we want long term over what we want in the moment. Our brain is wired for pleasure, safety, and efficiency. To be purposeful in your actions, you must be clear on your values and priorities so that you can take consistent action in support of your future vision.

Feelings to Fuel Action

Our emotions play a key role in building an aligned business. Remember, our beliefs (thoughts) create our feelings, which then fuel our actions, which then produce our results. Taking note of how you *want* to feel is a crucial step because how you feel directly translates to how you show up for yourself, for others, and for your business. Consider how your actions vary when you approach a task feeling at ease versus stressed. What about when you approach a client presentation when you are feeling confident versus feeling self-doubt? The way we choose to think about our day, and the way that choice makes us feel, directly impacts how we experience our life. Take a moment now to complete the following exercise.

Identify the top three emotions that you want to feel throughout the day. Here is a list of positive feelings to get you started.

Creative, motivated, committed, inspired, determined, confident, certain, energized, at ease, excited, open, empowered, prepared, engaged, centered, balanced, vibrant, joyful, dynamic, focused

Notice how each of the emotions (and the opposite emotion)

feels in your body.

If you were feeling (insert desired emotion in the blank)_____, what types of actions would you take in your business?

What results would these actions produce in your business?

How would showing up this way ripple into your personal and business life?

Get Specific to Get Results

Now that we have explored the various aspects of an aligned business, it is time to create your ideal life and business vision. The more specific you are, the better. Below are some prompts to get you started. Take time with this task and start to paint the vision for yourself. Make it so clear in your head that you can picture yourself stepping into that life from where you are today.

Imagine your dream business. How would you describe it?

What types of projects are you working on, and what are the budgets?

What makes you excited to come to work?

How do you spend your days?

Where do you do your work? Describe the environment.

Do you have a partner or employees?

How much money are you making?

What are your working hours?

How do you envision your business supporting your life?

What are you doing when you aren't at work?

How do you describe your lifestyle?

How do you stay creatively inspired?

What are your nonnegotiable activities that support your overall well-being?

Design Your Business As If. . .

Just as a new home must begin with pouring the foundation, an aligned business must be established with the proper support structure. The optimal configuration allows you to build your aligned business based on what you actually want, rather than reacting to what you do not want. Implementing changes and establishing your course is much easier to do on the front end. Backtracking is never trouble-free. If you're already in a situation of backtracking, trust that it will never get easier than this moment to change your course.

Once you have your ideal life and business vision defined, it's time to design your business "as if" your vision has already been achieved. What I often see at this point is that entrepreneurs get excited by the vision they have created, but then immediately get bogged down thinking it's unrealistic. Or they become frustrated that the changes can't happen in a day. Being in a rush never serves you. Let me assure you that you do not need to have reached a certain point in business in order to start implementing your vision for an aligned business. There is no time better than the present.

A great place to start designing your business "as if" is by establishing your ideal schedule. For example, if you want to set your office hours to be 9:00 a.m.-3:00 p.m., start putting those parameters in place now. Block off your calendar, decide when the last appointment of the day will be, and have a plan in place to transition out of work and on to the rest of your day.

Who Are You Becoming?

Just like the boat that is always is motion, we as humans are as well. We are always becoming *something*. We are becoming more of who we already are, or we are becoming more of who we want to be. Think about and answer the following questions.

Who are you becoming today, and are you being intentional about it? Why or why not?

How will this impact your life and business in six months, one year, or five years?

One of my favorite ways to practice becoming the next best version of yourself is by tapping into the wisdom of your future self. Your future self is more evolved and has solved the problems and challenges that you will encounter along the way to creating an aligned business. Most importantly, she (or he) has perspective.

I want you to imagine and visualize yourself as the person who has everything that you want. If this exercise seems difficult, you can even imagine yourself as a character you are studying to perform in an upcoming play. Then, take the time to answer the following questions.

What advice would that person tell you?

What does that person want you to know or understand?

List three ways that you are already living as this future version of yourself.

List three ways that you can begin to lean into being the person who creates your version of success.

What's the biggest difference between where you are now and where you want to be? What do you need to let go of? What will you bring forward?

Allow the Process to Unfold

The most important thing to remember during all of this planning and decision-making is that creating an aligned business is not a linear process. You might encounter unexpected obstacles, you might fall back into old habits, and your path might include many stepping stones that you could never have imagined. Acknowledge and remain open to your plan being a process, one that will need adjustment as you see it take shape.

As you move along the journey of creating an aligned business, find a way to keep your vision top of mind. Whether you hang this work on your inspiration board or plan a time to read through it regularly, the more we remind our brain of where we are headed, the more intentional we can be about getting there. Regular focus will set you up to see opportunities and make decisions that will move you forward. What's really incredible is that as you mentally rehearse your vision coming to fruition, you are actually changing the way your brain works. When you visualize your ideal life and business, your brain doesn't differentiate between reality and what you imagine. In essence, our mental rehearsal allows our thoughts and beliefs to become our reality. Here are a few helpful questions to stay on track in the process.

How will you remind yourself of your vision?

How will you know you're on track to creating your vision?

What can you do today to move closer to your vision tomorrow?

Trust that if you keep working to achieve your objectives, you will figure out the "how" along the way. The only way you won't is if you stop. I encourage you throughout your day to keep coming back to the experience that you want to create and remind yourself to make intentional choices. Remember your "why" and actively cultivate the elevated emotions you want to experience on a regular basis. You don't need to get there all at once; you simply need to be committed to growing, evolving, and believing in your ability to create exactly what you want.

*I mentioned my **aha!** moment when I met Desi and learned about her work. I had a different kind of **aha!** moment in 2016 when Kae Whitaker was on the show her first time. Before this, I didn't understand branding and why it had become such a buzz word. At that point, Window Works had been successful for 30-plus years, and we never once had a discussion on "branding." Through Kae, though, I learned we did have a brand at Window Works. Somehow, we had created it by instinct, by being who we are and conducting business in the way we did. It was one of the many lessons Kae would teach me over the next several years.*

Following that conversation with Kae and because of her, we leaned into our brand. We called it out in advertising and in our sales consultations. The result? We began to get more and more of our ideal projects each year and fewer and fewer of the wrong projects. Thank you, Kae!

I mention this example because you are likely in one of two camps now. Reading Desi's advice feels right and familiar, like it did to me. You already get it, and her strategies make it all the clearer, helping you get back to a mindset you already knew. Or you are like me when I spoke with Kae. This is all new, new ideas, new information. Maybe, on reflection, you find you are sort of doing some of these things, but now it's crystal clear how important it is to know what you want before you can begin to create it. Now, you can consciously and intentionally put the strategies to work for you.

So, what's next? It is time for you to create a business and a life that are in alignment with your dream for yourself and your future. The first step is to be clear on what results you want. Fuzzy and iffy won't cut it.

Getting and keeping clarity shouldn't be that difficult. Years ago, we got a dog, a Bichon Frise, for our daughter. I had German Shepherds and a Doberman growing up, and I remembered them being very obedient. You said "sit," they sat; you said "come," they came. Ahh, but this little Bichon was a scatter brain. He couldn't figure out what he wanted to do, much less what I wanted him to do. So, I hired a dog trainer.

Two things stand out all these years later. On the first lesson, the trainer explained, "You think my purpose is to train Luc, but the truth is, I am here to train you. Your dog wants to do what you want him to do. He is a pack animal, and he is in search of his Alpha. When you are his Alpha, he will do whatever you want."

The second thing he said was, "He is a dog. He does not actually understand English—although he can learn to associate the sounds he hears with the behaviors you want. But for him to do this, you must be very clear and stay consistent in your delivery and tone."

For example, he said, when we want a dog to sit, we don't say: "Hi Luc, sit boy, yes, baby, right here, sit by mommy, be a good dog, come on now. This is too many sounds, words. He cannot compute this. He doesn't speak English."

For results, we say: **Luc, sit.**

The Universe works the same way. When you are not sure of your business and life goals, you send the Universe too many words, too much noise. Fuzzy goals to the Universe are like 18-word commands to a dog.

You are the Alpha in your life. For results, decide what you want, declare it, focus on it, and be consistent in your actions. It works, with business, relationships, and dogs.

Once you know what you want, you need to build a strategy to achieve your vision. It may take a hot minute or a decade to get there, but that's okay. The time is going to pass by either way. I like Desi's suggestion for accountability. She encourages us to ask our future self, "What do you think about how I spent this day today?" Try it. It is a powerful reminder to keep yourself on target.

Big dreams, big goals take time. Just like Luc didn't sit, stay, or do much else I wanted him to do, at the beginning. But he learned soon enough to listen to me. The Vin Man would say, "He only obeys you." I tried for years to get Vin to see I was the only one who spoke to him clearly, with consistency, and with an expectation of results. The rest of them, well, they talked "noise" at Luc.

If you have a dream for your life and your business, follow Desi's *advice. Do her exercises. Train yourself to communicate with the Universe with clarity and intention. Trust the process. Trust that you can create anything you put your mind to. Trust that you are the Alpha in your own life.*

-LN

About the Author

Desi Creswell is a Certified Life and Business Coach who helps interior designers stop feeling overwhelmed so they can intentionally achieve next-level success with more freedom and fulfillment. An awarding-winning interior designer who has worked for world-renowned design and architecture firms prior to establishing her own design practice, Desi is uniquely equipped to empower her clients with an essential blend of industry specific expertise and mindset coaching. Her passion is to help designers build thriving businesses that enrich and support their lives as a whole.

Desi Creswell has been a featured guest on A *Well-Designed Business®* podcast episodes 475 and 557.

CHAPTER 9

Eileen Hahn

reating a profitable business is a major undertaking. It takes a tremendous amount of dedication and work, and in itself is a worthy goal. But do you want more than success, more than profits? Do you want to own a business that, as Eileen says, is exceptional?

Eileen's mission is to help you build an amazing business, not an average business. A place where everyone loves their work and loves to be there. The kind of business whose team members feel accomplished, feel valued, and who work together, enthusiastically, toward shared goals. Fair warning, this kind of business does not happen because **you** are happy and excited to be there. To create this, well...**you must create it.** You must lead your company, not simply own it.

If you have read my first book or have attended any of my live keynotes, you know having a clear mission and vision for your company is the first thing I talk about. Believing in having these defined from the start has served both Window Works and A Well-Designed Business® podcast quite well. Eileen and I agree—110 percent—this is the first step. You must know who you are, why you do what you do, whom you will do it for, and how you will do it.

On the podcast #545, Laurel Smith described her first year in business. Troubled by both indecision and wrong decisions, she struggled to find her footing. She recalled how she read in my book the advice to begin with your company mission and core values. She also described how she brushed over this advice, in a hurry, to get to the other chapters. Later, in hindsight, she understood how many of the dilemmas she faced were a result of skipping this step. You could hear the joy in her voice as she described her new company mission and core values. Now, decision-making is easier because she knows what she wants and where she is going.

Would you ever dream of selecting furnishings for a client before you saw and measured the space? Of course not. Beautiful furnishings, without consideration of size, style, or function, are of no value to the success of the design. Know this: Your design talent, your passion and love for the industry, are the same as the beautiful furnishings. Without a specific vision, mission, and plan, your talent is of no value to the success of your business.

An exceptional business coach and mentor, especially in the areas of personal and team development, Eileen has been incredibly impactful on both of my businesses.

In this chapter, Eileen outlines five more important steps to take. This means none of us can pat ourselves on the back and say, "I have my mission, vision, and values down. Check." We must push ourselves to go further and commit to the other five key steps. I know from firsthand experience this is not easy, but it does work, and it is worth it.

Read her advice, take notes, think deeply and carefully, and **don't skip any steps.**

–LN

How to Grow and Scale Your Design Firm

Eileen Hahn

You love design, color, architecture, creating a mood, eliciting an emotion, making a room come to life. You have a great idea for your design business that you're really excited about. You're passionate about this work. You know that you can't do it alone. You need help. In fact, you need a team of people working together with you to accomplish your goals.

You decide to hire a team: A design assistant, a junior designer, a bookkeeper, etc. Your team is hired and working, but there are problems. Maybe you don't have the right people for the jobs. No one is as passionate about the business as you are. People are working, putting in the time, but things aren't going well. Some of the team are not on the same page as you in terms of how to execute their job. They don't share your values, ethics, and viewpoint about teamwork, customer service, and professionalism. Details are falling through the cracks. On top of all that, you're not achieving the sales and profit results you'd hoped for, and you're not sure how to do so. As if that weren't enough, everyone wants a raise! No one feels like they're being paid enough, and employees are bickering with each other, causing friction and an unpleasant work environment.

What to do?

Six Business Fundamentals to Help Your Organization Excel

In my 25 years of leadership consulting, I've discovered six crucial principles of thriving businesses and have seen how those fundamentals work to eliminate certain repetitive issues that surface in a variety of different businesses. The methodologies are time-tested, best practices for design firms, small entrepreneurial businesses as well as for Fortune 500 organizations. The spectrum of highly successful businesses has these fundamentals in place; they are part of the daily operating procedure, business cycle, and culture.

The good news is that you don't have to know the six business fundamentals in advance or even have a strong idea of how to execute them. You can easily build your skills and learn to integrate these essential principles into your organization over time so that they become clear and obvious. Once you do, you will wonder how you ever lived without them! They are:

1. Compelling vision

Your vision is clear, "alive," and compelling. In sharing it with your team, you inspire them to take action to reach your vision. Together, you climb the mountain and achieve your goals.

2. Actionable values

Company values are your footholds as you move toward your vision. You set them, model them and hold yourself and your team accountable to them. They guide your day-to-day operations.

3. Strategic and annual business plan

Strategic and annual business plans are the road map used to reach your vision. You foster innovation and improvement as part of that process. Remember, there is always room for growth and improvement.

4.   Cohesive team

You establish trust with each team member and demonstrate that you care about them. Once the individual connections are made, you then bring the team together to work as a collective. You take time to communicate and bond with your team regularly.

5.   Clearly defined roles and accountability

You have defined roles, responsibility, accountability, and exceptional performance. All of those details provide clarity, focus, and comfort to your employees, as well as a tangible set of instructions that helps them excel at their job.

6.   Coaching and feedback that honors each individual

You are committed to helping your team grow and develop as human beings, and you provide professional development. You ask for their input and tap into their creativity and personal superpowers.

You may read that list and say, "Well, I do all or most of that!" It's true that many companies do, to some extent. But if you are still having some of the challenges that I mentioned earlier, it may be that you are not practicing all of the fundamentals and diving deeply into each. For example, on the surface, you can check the boxes that say you already have a vision and values statement. Maybe it is posted on your website or in your office, but your employees don't know it and aren't living it.

Don't worry if that's the case, we'll get you to where you need to be.

The Secret Sauce: Leading with Love

This chapter asks you questions about the current state of your business as well as where you'd like to be. It outlines best practices for each of the business fundamentals and provides the key ingredient or special sauce: leading with love.

What does *leading with love* mean?

It means caring deeply about your employees—not just about their engagement and your bottom line, but about all aspects of who they are in their lives. Leading with love is not just about showing your team your best self, but also encouraging *them* to be their best selves and supporting their success. It means taking the time to listen from a place of attentive compassion. It means being honest and offering constructive criticism because you know it can help them to improve their work, achieve success, and enhance their long-term career. Leading with love also requires being humble enough to listen to your team's feedback and incorporating any changes that could make for a better work environment and a greater sense of engagement.

Now, let's get into the fundamentals so that you can begin putting them into tangible practice!

Compelling Vision

A strong vision will fuel positive behavior and performance in your team members. It will also attract talent and motivate current employees to perform their best work—a key ingredient of successful organizations aligned with exceptional employees.

In fact, research from Microsoft reveals that 88 percent of millennials (who make up the majority of the current workforce) said that selecting a company with a strong mission/values system was important to them. Likewise, evidence is growing that people across generations are looking for greater meaning and the potential to make a big contribution through their work.

If you have well-defined values and a clear vision, employees not only observe such characteristics, but also purposely seek them. Make those fundamentals evident on your website, marketing materials, and within your organization.

What does a compelling, ennobled vision look like in a design firm?

Gensler: to create a better world through the power of design.

Inspired Interiors: curate spaces that embolden you to enjoy life in new, empowering ways.

Blakely Interior Design: to inspire the world to live vibrantly in their homes and in their everyday lives.

Brown: to create a memorable brand experience for our clients while enhancing the quality of life for all we serve.

By articulating your vision in a clear and succinct way, you can attract high performers and unite your team under the umbrella of a powerful guiding principle. Simply stated, if you want to get people to climb a mountain, you must tell them what's on top of the mountain and get them excited about it. They will feel enthused by the vision and will have the assurance that their contribution is valuable and appreciated. They will cultivate a greater sense of meaning and purpose, which will give them the incentive to wake up every day, excited and ready to navigate the challenges and rewards of the day ahead. Think about it: Work takes up the majority of most people's lives. When we are lucky enough to have a purpose that touches our hearts and unites us under a common goal, we will naturally be motivated to achieve great things.

Once you establish the vision, it isn't enough to assume that everyone already knows it. It needs to be repeated often and should be posted in a prominent place for all employees to see. Discuss it regularly at individual and company meetings. When necessary, update it and ensure that all annual and strategic plans are working toward achieving it.

See how your honest answers to the following questions compare to the emphatic "yes!" that each should elicit:

- Is your vision an ennobled future state so compelling that your employees are excited to come into the office every day and work toward achieving it?
- Does your entire team know the vision? Could they recite it?
- Does each employee know how important their role is in attaining the vision?
- Are your annual goals and strategic plan designed to help you achieve the vision?

Actionable Values

Company values are necessary footholds as you move toward your vision. They also aid in attracting and retaining employees, which many organizations find difficult. Values serve as guiding principles for how to behave in life and on the job. They shape how we respond to others—customers, team members, associates, etc., and govern the cadence of our personal and professional lives, with great impact on our levels of personal satisfaction and reward.

Here are San Francisco design firm Form+Field's values:

Radical Transparency

- We're direct and honest in our communication to each other, our clients, and collaborators.
- We freely and openly share and discuss information, ideas, opinions, and disagreements.
- We promptly bring challenges and issues to light and admit mistakes.
- We treat people with respect.

Independent Thinking

- We're curious, open-minded, and love to learn new things.
- We seek alternative perspectives and feedback in order to push boundaries.
- We take the initiative in seeking the best solution for a given situation, questioning what we know and not relying on past experience or how others do it.
- We continuously look for new ways to improve our work and processes to enable us to perform our best work.

Service-Oriented Adaptability

- We seek to understand our clients and collaborators and how best to work with them.
- We value flexibility in crafting solutions that maintain our high level of service and quality.
- We respond to changing conditions and opportunities, updating processes and priorities to what's most crucial and valuable for the company at any given time.
- We do whatever tasks are necessary to help the company even if it's not in our job description.
- When given new information or perspective, we're open to changing our minds and previously made decisions to get to the right decision.

Healthy Community

- We inspire each other with our tenacity, optimism, and passion for design, service, and excellence.
- We seek what is best for our company and colleagues, while taking into consideration individual needs and boundaries.
- We make decisions based on the long term, identifying the root causes of issues and treating the root causes, not just the symptoms.
- We are engaged with and contribute to our broader community in and outside of the design industry.

Being a part of a company with values like the ones stated above contributes to a positive, enlivening, empowering experience.

Your values also set the stage for your company culture, which becomes the behaviors and attitudes that leaders and employees demonstrate and live every day—namely, kindness, collaboration, respect, and a safe and nurturing work environment. When employees and leaders tell me that a toxic or negative culture exists in their midst, the reason often is because company values have not been identified—or the leaders of the organization are not explicitly living these values, regularly discussing them, and holding employees accountable to them. With clearly defined values that leaders and employees are actively modeling, the culture flourishes and becomes solid and strong.

Your honest answers to the following questions will pinpoint areas where you are or aren't succeeding:

- Are your values clear and well-defined?
- Do employees know what specific behaviors correspond to these values?
- Are your leaders and employees living your company's values every day?

- Do the values feel "alive" in the organization, and are they pivotal to daily operations?
- Does the interview and selection process require choosing employees aligned with these values?
- Are employees held accountable to living the values?
- Do you recognize and applaud team members who are living the values?
- Is it addressed immediately when someone acts outside the values?
- Do you talk about the values regularly at company meetings and team retreats?

How to Create a Shared Vision and Values

The first two business fundamentals—compelling vision and actionable values—are absolutely pivotal when it comes to gathering a team that is strong and motivated. In order to put the first two fundamentals for leading with love into practice in your company, follow this set of actions:

1. Take time to personally reflect on what you would like the future of your team and organization to look like. Think big, bold, "anything is possible." Brainstorm about a potential future state until something inside you stirs and you feel a strong desire to work toward that vision. Jot down values that you believe will guide you to reach your vision—values that are *essential* to reaching that vision. As the leader of your company, or your team, you always want to start with *your* vision and values first.

2. Next, invite your team to work with you to establish a shared vision and values that all of you can support and exhibit. Explain the purpose and benefits of having a clear and

compelling vision and values. Show them examples of successful company visions and values and ask them to think it through and come to your next meeting prepared to discuss their own ideas for a shared vision and values.

3. At your next meeting, have each person share their vision and values. Perhaps you'll choose to write them down on a flipchart for everyone to see; then, discuss them, expand on them, brainstorm together, and piggyback on each other's ideas. Add your vision and values into the team ideas. Many times, you'll find that some of your ideas overlap with those of your team members. After the team discusses all the ideas, each person should identify the vision and values that most resonate with them.

4. Next, focus on the key vision and values that your team identified. Discuss them as a group with the intent of outlining a common shared vision and values. Come to a consensus on your shared vision and values.

5. Have another meeting to finalize, solidify, and commit to the new vision and values. At this meeting, talk about how you are going to achieve that vision and how the agreed-upon values look like in action on the job every day.

6. Post the vision and values, talk about them regularly, live them, and celebrate them.

Strategic and Annual Business Plan

Having a clear, well-thought-out plan based on data analysis and input from multiple sources and constituents will set the targets that are necessary to help you achieve your vision. Take time each year to conduct analysis and develop annual goals with your team, as this will dramatically increase your annual and long-term results.

A strategic/annual plan defines where your organization is going, the steps to take to get there, the expected outcomes and results, and metrics to measure success. It is important to conduct both internal and external scanning as part of your planning process.

External scanning includes:

- Macro environment: What impact is the current economy and world market having on your business? What are the local, national, and global projections and trends?
- Industry: what are the industry trends, challenges, changes, and opportunities at hand?
- Competition: What is the current state of affairs with your competition? What do you know about them and their strategies?
- Industry leaders and role models: What are they doing that is making them so effective? What have they started doing? Stopped doing? What can you learn from them?
- Customers: What do your customers want today? What are they buying and/or not buying, and why?

Internal scanning includes:

- Financial review: how has your business performed over multiple years?
- Sales and product analysis: how have your product(s) and business performed in various markets over multiple years?
- Employee data: What are your data findings on factors such as turnover/retention, time to hire, employee

engagement, exit interviews? Do you have a leadership continuity or succession plan?

- Analysis of business-generation methods and their effectiveness: which business-generating methods produce the highest sales volume?
- Internal processes and systems: which of your systems are or aren't working well?
- Distinctive competencies: What makes your organization unique? What does your organization/team do particularly well?

After your planning team reviews all that data together, conduct a **S**trengths, **W**eaknesses, **O**pportunities, and **T**hreats (SWOT) analysis to identify your organization's standing. From that analysis, you can look for themes that arise and use those themes to develop annual goals and strategies.

Organizations achieve consistently higher results when leaders take the time to analyze their business and take positive steps together as a team to create and implement a specific plan.

A well-developed plan should be shared with employees and reviewed on a quarterly basis for progress. Your entire team should know the plan and goals; be focused on the plan and goals; take positive action to achieve them; review progress; and make course corrections as necessary. All of those actions build confidence and a sense of purpose in achieving your company's vision and values.

Having a clear, well-thought-out plan, based on data analysis and input from multiple sources and constituents, will set the targets necessary to help you achieve your vision and dramatically increase your annual and long-term results.

Laura Umansky, founder of Laura U Interior Designs, credits

annual strategic planning and quarterly planning meetings with her leadership team as a critical component that enabled her to scale her business to $5 million and more. Each year she meets for two days offsite to do annual planning with her leadership team as well as meeting one day each quarter to review progress and make adjustments. She uses the Entrepreneurs Operating System (EOS) to track and monitor her goals.

Answer the following questions honestly to compare your hands-on involvement to your current level of success:

- Do you have annual goals? Do all employees know the goals, and are they working to achieve them?
- Do your annual goals include financial, operations, customers, employees, technology, and innovation?
- Do you take one to two days each year to conduct internal and external scans and data analysis before setting your annual goals?
- Do you carefully consider whom to involve in the planning process, including specific team members and external consultants?
- Do you periodically review the plan and overall progress to goals in leadership and employee meetings?

Cohesive Team

Building a cohesive team starts with establishing trust with each team member and demonstrating that you care about them. Meeting one-on-one with team members to discuss their work, their personal and professional goals and aspirations, their skills and professional development all come into play. When you take time away from the regular workday to have these personal meetings, you are honoring the employees and letting them know that they are important. You want to help them grow and develop. You take the time to ask questions, listen, and provide guidance and support to help them attain their goals. While your focus is on the employee, every good leader is skillful at eliciting feedback. For example, you can ask them if you can do anything to help them in their role. You can also inquire about the efficacy of your style and encourage them to let you know what you could do differently. Once those individual connections are made, you can then bring the team together to work as a collective.

Developing a cohesive team includes talking about and fostering an open, supportive, transparent team environment. Don't just assume you already know what that ideal looks like: Ask your team members what it would look like to them. Involve them in creating norms and agreements that are necessary in order to operate smoothly as a team.

As the leader, you must speak about the importance of teamwork, set goals with the team with their input and participation, and recognize positive collaborative team behavior. When the team reaches its goals, mark the occasion by celebrating together. When the team is struggling, you can bring them together and let them know you support them and that you will meet the challenges as a team. You, as the leader, are there to support them and to encourage them to support each other in attaining your agreed-upon goals.

Many high-performing teams that I work with have regular gatherings, including annual performance reviews, opportunities to share what is and isn't working, and an overall SWOT analysis examining the strengths, weaknesses, and opportunities of each member's specific function in the company. Based on that information, the team sets their annual goals by examining both the functional goals that they want to achieve as a team and the ways in which they work together to achieve these goals. All team members commit to the goals and agree to support each other in reaching them. The teams usually set up check-ins monthly, quarterly, or for key milestones to ensure they are on track. Many will have mini-celebrations when they hit key milestones. Team lunches, dinners, happy hours, softball games, game nights, and other team-building activities can help to establish a sense of camaraderie, community, and enjoyment.

As the leader, your key roles are to set the vision, support the team with resources, provide feedback, recognize and reward excellence, and address individual and team issues as they arise. Sometimes a team loses its cohesiveness when one or more team members behave in a manner that is not supportive of the team. That setback can include acting out of alignment with the company values, bad-mouthing a team member, putting team members down, embarrassing or humiliating a team member, refusing to help other teammates, or refusing to attend important team functions. If other team members don't address that hindrance directly with the team member then it's your job as a leader to step in and meet with the team member(s) to compassionately listen to their concerns and address the issue. You can share the importance of living the company values and working in a positive and supportive manner with the team.

Use your honest answers to the following questions to determine your effectiveness as a caring leader:

- Do you meet one-on-one with your direct reports and talk about their work, goals, skills, personal and professional goals, and aspirations?
- Do you routinely discuss the value and importance of teamwork? Have you set team goals?

- Do you recognize and reward teamwork and team successes?
- Have you used an anonymous employee survey to find out if individuals feel honored, respected, and cared for?

Clearly Defined Roles and Accountability

Defining roles, responsibility, accountability, and what an exceptional job looks like can provide clarity, focus, and comfort to your employees. All of those details provide a tangible set of instructions that helps employees excel at their job.

People often ask me what questions to ask when they interview for a new job. I often suggest the following:

- What does an exceptional job look like in this role?
- What results are you hoping for the person in this role to achieve?
- How does this role fit into achieving the company's annual goals and vision?

Those questions are great to ask a potential manager, but they can also be asked of current employees. Do they know the answers as they relate to their respective jobs? Do you? Have you talked about it? If you have not spoken specifically about what an exceptional job looks like in their role and you see that they are not being exceptional today, then address it immediately.

Many exceptional, high-performing teams have found it helpful to update their job descriptions, deliverables, accountabilities, and expectations for exceptional performance and to share them with other team members in a meeting. Often, they will notice overlap between roles, as well as gaps where team members are experiencing challenges, taking on tasks that are not part of their job description, or allowing tasks to fall through the cracks. Together, as a team, you can discuss how to best approach all of those experiences and further clarify roles and responsibilities.

I have found that most people want to do an exceptional job. They do the best they can until something tells them otherwise. When people know what exceptional looks like, their performance is elevated. Often, when leaders find that their employees are not doing well, I encourage them to go through a checklist of potential reasons:

- Does the employee know what to do and what is expected of them?
- Do they have the skill set to do the job?
- Do they receive ongoing coaching to develop their skills?

Accountability works best when people are encouraged to be accountable to themselves, to the team, and to their manager. It seldom works when managers attempt to hold employees accountable, as that approach can feel like micromanaging. It's always best when team members are motivated and proactive about their own performance.

Sounds easy, right? But how exactly do you set up that type of accountability? It starts with clearly defining expectations, goals, and results for each person in their position (i.e., accountability to themselves). Then, they can share that with the team (i.e., accountability to the team). With that information in hand, they can be asked to report to their manager weekly, monthly, or quarterly on their performance and achievements (i.e., accountability to the manager).

Managers and leaders must also display a sense of accountability to their employees by staying abreast of their progress and offering them resources on how to do even better. They can ask such questions as, "How are you doing? How is it going? Where are you in relation to meeting your goals? What kind of support do you feel that you need in doing so?"

The employee will learn that they can expect such questions and will be ready with answers. If it still feels like they are not meeting expectations or goals, the leader's role is to provide them with the support, resources, and training that are necessary in order for them to get there.

Design firm Corey Damen Jenkins & Associates has clearly defined job descriptions and expectations that guide his team members in their job and also provide a road map for job growth and development. Employees know exactly what is expected of them in their current role and if they want to move to another position they know the skills, responsibilities, and performance expectations there are for that position as well.

Your honest answers to the following questions will show if you engender accountability:

- Are employees clear about their roles and responsibilities?
- Are any tasks falling through the cracks?
- Are your job descriptions up to date and utilized? How often are they reviewed and updated?
- What does accountability look like within your organization? Do you hold your team members accountable? Are they accountable to themselves and each other?

Coaching and Feedback That Honors Each Individual

As a leader, you have the opportunity to be instrumental in the growth, development, and well-being of your team. It starts with genuinely caring about your people and knowing their strengths and weaknesses. Value the professional and personal development of each employee, and then make a commitment to being the kind of leader who takes time to develop and coach your staff. At Martha O'Hara Interiors employees receive positive and constructive feedback and coaching each week in one-on-one meetings. This employee development is an essential piece of the company culture that CEO Kate O'Hara describes as "a community of lifelong learners, people who want to improve and continue to grow on an on-going basis."

Training and employee development can come in many forms and modalities, from training developed both by managers and team members to working with external trainers to providing opportunities for professional development via webinars, books, podcasts, online courses, conferences, and workshops. Make your offerings fun, engaging, and innovative—and ask for feedback on their effectiveness.

It's important to note that professional development can occur both individually and as a team. Be sure to have one-on-one conversations with your employees and work with them to improve their individual performance and enhance their professional skills. You might also encourage them to learn and develop skills in an area outside of their current responsibilities in order to foster their growth, curiosity, and engagement—and to prepare them to take on greater tasks and responsibilities as a part of their continuous development.

Answer the following questions honestly to determine how your employees might judge your interest in them:

- Do you know each employee's strengths, superpowers, areas/opportunities for development?

- When was the last time that you had a conversation with them about all of the above?
- Are you actively working with each employee to develop and enhance specific skills?
- What professional development activities do you provide? Support? Reimburse?

Your Next Steps to Lead with Love

Now that you have reviewed the six business fundamentals and engaged in some powerful introspection about your own practices (including what you are doing well and where you can seek to improve), you're ready to lead with love!

If you approach leadership with love and care, you will make a huge difference in both your employees' lives and your bottom line. Studies show that employees who feel cared about perform at a higher level—and what's more, they will stay.

I know this to be true: to be better at something, you must be around those who are better than you at it.

That is why, despite nearly four decades in business, I learn something about being a better leader from Eileen every darn week. She helps me see when I have brushed aside some of the other steps.

Through Eileen's counsel, I have learned the problems we encounter with employees often have way less to do with them and much more to do with our leadership.

You know how whenever you are having trouble with a client or a vendor, I urge you to rewind the situation to pinpoint the moment you personally could have changed the outcome? Likewise, Eileen identifies how issues with employees can usually be traced right back to us as leaders. Typically, we ignore or we misunderstand how our poor management or lack of management affects our team. Eileen's advice always provides the perspective to see the actual problem, rather than the perceived problem.

I know effective leadership is essential to success. I also know Eileen would elaborate: Inspired leadership is essential to job satisfaction. Inspired leadership fosters joyfulness, productivity, and achievement, which results in exceptional success.

What do you think? Are you feeling motivated to lead and operate an exceptional business?

I urge you to take the lessons from both Eileen and Laurel Smith. Do not pass go, stop, or collect your $200. Do the leadership work necessary to craft the business you desire.

If you combine skillful leadership with your passion and talent and, as Eileen says, lead with love, you will be a force to be reckoned with. You will shine light and joy into the world, making it more beautiful, one client at a time.

This is a wonderful thing. I hope you will do it. The rest of us need you to do it.

-LN

About the Author

Eileen Hahn is a leadership consultant who works with firms like Anheuser-Busch, Ericsson Worldwide, General Motors, the San Diego Padres, interior design firms, and smaller entrepreneurial firms. She teaches leaders how to hire and lead exceptional employees to achieve high levels of performance. Eileen's work has improved productivity, profitability, employee work passion, and joy.

Eileen Hahn has been a featured guest on A *Well-Designed Business*® podcast episode 363 and 589.

CONCLUSION

LuAnn Nigara

So much goodness has come into my life through A *Well-Designed Business*® podcast. At this time, with over 600 interviews, the conversations, the lessons, the aha! moments, the laughs, and the tears—*of joy*—are stacked high to the ceiling, *and I love every minute of it.*

We have met each other at industry events, at *LuAnn Live*, at Power Talk Friday Tours, and through my coaching and courses. Every day, in every way, I am impressed by your stories of growth, transformation, resilience, and success.

Together, we have created a community of interior designers, industry partners, and creatives in adjunct fields such as architects, builders, photographers, landscape architects, writers, graphic artists, and web developers. Every one of us has come together to teach, lead, share, and support each other in our singular goal: To create a prosperous business that we are proud of. A business that enhances not only our lives, but also the lives of the clients who we serve.

It humbles me and touches me when you thank me with

your huge hugs, your heartfelt emails, and your hand-written notes. Here's the thing: I know the magic really comes from my guests—the men and women who have come on the show with an open mind and an open heart, sharing their experience and their expertise so that we can benefit. With every conversation, they gift us with a strategy, with some advice, with that missing section of the road map that guides us in our journey to operate our business more efficiently, more profitably.

This series of books, A *Well-Designed Business®: The Power Talk Friday Experts*, is the materialization of this magic because at the core of this tremendous body of knowledge are the recurring guests whom I have named my Power Talk Friday Experts. Each of these savvy people possesses, as Liam Neeson says, a very particular set of skills. Through those skills, we have gained an insight, an idea, a strategy that has propelled our business. In my opinion, few things are more contagious, more inspiring, than a person who is so evidently passionate about helping others achieve the same success they have enjoyed. What captures me is the synthesis of achievement, skill, talent, and experience, compounded by the joy and excitement of sharing it. I am compelled to keep inviting them into our community. Put simply, when I discover these special people, I hang onto them.

Within this volume, we have met the standouts of the last year, individuals whose personal mission it is to help us be better business people. In truth, they are among the many who have inspired me to be a better business person.

These professionals, along with the professionals in volume I, have imparted the power, the information, the tools you need to create dramatic change in your business. There is one catch, though. You must be willing to *do* more than read; you must be willing to do. I have brought them to you. They have stepped up to share their expertise. What happens next is up to you.

At this point, I encourage you to go back and, if you haven't already, take notes. Give each chapter some additional thought. Then, please, commit to diving in at a deeper level. Start with whichever chapter you choose. My advice? Ask yourself, which chapter gave you a stomach punch? You know exactly the one I am talking about—the one that while reading it, you kept saying to yourself, "This is me. I need to do this!"

Go there, tackle that chapter immediately.

Dedicate the time you need to make the biggest change or the hardest change, first. Maybe you can do it yourself, maybe you will need to reach out to the coauthor for help, or to a designer bestie for accountability. Just do whatever it takes to make the change. The change that you knew you needed, as you read that chapter. Don't think about how hard it will be. Think only about how proud of yourself you will be on the other side.

Remember what Executive Vice President of Walt Disney World Operations Lee Cockerell told us in podcast episode #222? Lee said, "When you do the hard thing, everything else gets easier. But when you only do the easy things, everything else gets harder."

This wisdom has served me very well throughout my entire life, long before I met Lee. But Lee stated the sentiment so directly, so clearly, that now what rings in my head, almost daily, are his words. If you apply this insight to your business, there is no possibility of not being successful. (Yes, that's an intentional double negative.)

So, take on the hardest lessons for you in this book, and everything will get easier. In fact, would you do something for me? Document the process of tackling the lessons in this book—

track the changes you make in your business and the results you achieve. Then send your list of The Things I Learned From A *Well-Designed Business®* to me in an email so I can invite you to be on the podcast, where we will share your work and your success with our community! Deal?

So, here we go...

It's straight talk, and it's action! Are you ready? Go get started!

LuAnn Nigara

Made in the USA
Monee, IL
04 February 2021